Abundantly You!
On Purpose In
Business

*Growing and Prospering In Business
From Within*

Advance Praise

I would like to thank you for writing this book. The authors this time around have done it again—on a business level. Personally, it has helped me do business and work in a new way. While the concepts are time tested, having them presented and implemented in a cohesive manner, made a huge shift in my new approach. Job well done!

> ~ **Karen Adams**, M. A., Counselor for Montgomery County Public Schools

As an entrepreneur, I found this book not only refreshing, but much needed in the marketplace. It's how I will proceed in all of my business endeavors moving forward. Cheers! for *Abundantly You! On Purpose in Business.*

> ~ **Sharon Zhamalu**, Entrepreneur | Z-Consulting

Abundantly You! will be a "game changer" to entrepreneurs everywhere. On the pages of this book readers will find probing questions and provocative responses to being "on purpose" in the business you lead. The contributors to this book, another of Antoinette Sykes' *Bounceback Series* have been through the tests and the fires; their stories will enlighten you and reinforce your understanding of abundance and the myriad ways it impacts and plays into your overall mastery of life.

Abundantly You! *is* a mix of complex, yet simple concepts... creating a new perspective of connecting our core values, business practices and awareness of being fully congruent with "life." It is, if you will, varied perspectives of turning practical life lessons into life shifts that will inspire change from the inside out. Antoinette Sykes is at her core a change agent; each of her books has been designed to open the minds of her readers to larger possibilities. Through her hand-picked contributors to the anthology, Antoinette opens the way for readers to follow myriad insights into human nature. Her books are proven tools to help stimulate a deeper understanding and provide step-by-step systems readers can use on the path to being Abundantly You! and on purpose in business.

Abundantly You! is a masterfully interwoven collective of anecdotes and expertise... simplifying the process of living life on the terms of big thinking and the kind of desires that represent abundance. You will not be able to read these stories without being inspired to act. At its core, the book is filled with common sense, positive reinforcement and specific advice—the words of wisdom—that are both inspirational and useful.

~ **T. R. Stearns**, EdS

Abundantly You! On Purpose In Business

Growing and Prospering In Business From Within

by

Antoinette Sykes

Davida Bratton

Anna Long

Shari Molchan

Lisa Marie Pepe

Dean Philpott

Valerie Sorrentino

Anna Weber

v

Requests to Dean Philpott for permission should be addressed to:
Philpott Seminars
Offices in:
Nanaimo, BC
Whitehorse, Yukon
Phone: 867-334-1234
E-mail: dean@deanphilpott.com

Limit of Liability Disclaimer of Warranty.
While the Publisher and author have used their best efforts in preparing this book, they make no representations or warranties with respect to the accuracy or completeness of this book and specifically disclaim any implied warranties of merchantability or fitness for a particular purpose. No warranty may be created or extended by sales representatives or written sales materials. The publisher and author are not engaged in rendering professional services, and you should consult with a professional where appropriate. Neither publisher nor author shall be liable for any loss or profit or other commercial damages, including but not limited to special, incidental, consequential or other damages.

Disclaimer: This book is a compilation of ideas from numerous experts who have each contributed a chapter. As such, the views expressed in each chapter are those of the contributors and not necessarily of the anthologist.

For general information on other books written by this author contact

Philpott Seminars
Offices in:
Nanaimo, BC
Whitehorse, Yukon
Phone: 867-334-1234
E-mail: dean@deanphilpott.com

ISBN-13: 978-0994748300 (Philpott Seminars)
ISBN-10: 0994748302

Printed in the United States of America
10 9 8 7 6 5 4 3 2 1

Cover design by Debra Breck I Deb Graphics

Dedication

This book is dedicated to you if you are searching for
a better way...
to do business and lead in the workplace.

Table of Contents

Foreword

The words of acclaimed author and publisher, Sarah Ban Breathnach, epitomize the collective stories found in *Abundantly You! On Purpose in Business.*

Whatever we are waiting for
—peace of mind, contentment, grace, the inner
awareness of simple abundance—
it will surely come to us, but only when we are ready
to receive it with an open and grateful heart.

~ Sarah Ban Breathnach (1947 -   )
Publisher and best-selling author.

Antoinette Sykes has "done it again!" with book number three in her Unsinkable series, by gathering together highly successful people who share their stories of success in finance, relationships and spirituality. The stories show how real is the belief: *although most everyone seeks a happier, more successful life, so few attain it.*

These stories are written to propose new ways of viewing and approaching success in business, and the abundance that normally accompanies it. Each story is written in a straightforward, surprisingly simple manner; each is written especially for entrepreneurs seeking success not only in terms of monetary gain, but tapping into the abundance found in relationships and spirituality.

Readers will see themselves in the stories, and will pick up on the writers' encouragement to realize life mistakes, come to terms with them, and turn bad choices into future victories.

The pages of this "must read" anthology are filled with solid advice to improve finances, connection, relationships and spirituality... taking a practical approach to create shifts not only in the mind, but in the actions of readers; action that will open hearts, minds and opportunities to be more abundant, and experience the rewards of a life of purpose.

Many of the contributing authors share wisdom and knowledge that comes from a direct relationship with whomever they see as their creator, and reveal their experiential fundamentals: a clear link between generating revenue and spirituality, as they encourage readers to focus not on money, but self-discipline, integrity and the personal depth of spirituality necessary to achieve prosperity and abundance.

Special focus is given to establishing positive attitudes toward money, and how each has adopted effective spiritual-based strategies.

There is indeed significant merit to this third publication, as Antoinette Sykes has taken readers through *Unsinkable*, which contained poignant stories of women who refused to let life keep them down, and then in *Miracles, Momentum and Manifestation*, where the stories helped readers take the "next" step and learn to recognize miracles in their lives, and use them as the momentum to manifest more of the same.

Somewhere, at some time in our life, if we are sincere in our quest for being abundant, not only in life, but in business, we must learn some of the messages found in *Abundantly You! On Purpose in Business.*

> Abundance is found in the uncommon hours as God's reward for how we develop relationships with others in our lives, and find our purpose in serving them.

> Personal development, in the pursuit of abundance calls for individual responsibility to create a life structured, and with healthy boundaries.

> Building a business "on purpose" is a process of personal transformation and consistent movement toward success... even in the face of fear and uncertainty.

Attaining wealth, well being, and knowing your life has purpose need not be a mystery! *Abundantly You!* identifies the areas where you will benefit from developing a new relationship with money, a new understanding of abundance, and a new pathway to build a business "on purpose."

Jacqueline VanCampen
Author, Writing Coach, Founder
www.wiseheartwithin.com

Acknowledgements

As a woman and business owner this book, as a component of the *Bounceback Series,* continues to be part of a dream come true—becoming an author and a best selling one, at that.

Many thanks to God for speaking to me so clearly; I love you.

My family and friends are simply the best. Know that your love, laughter and firm words of wisdom land warmly in my heart. For that, I am forever grateful for being connected. I genuinely like you and unabashedly love you.

To the miracles I have yet to meet, I know you're on the way. I'm simply giddy with love and expectation!

My literary team... well, you rock; that's all. Thank you.

Introduction

Go back with me a bit here. I clearly remember… it was one of those days in the workplace a few years ago, before I found myself a full time entrepreneur and spent valuable time wondering just why things were "off" in my efforts.

Deep thoughts, followed by some serious introspection crowded my mind…*Why am I frustrated at how I have to show up as one person, so to speak, and then feel so free to share all of me: My career expertise, my faith, my comedic nature and overall jovial self, with only some of my workplace colleagues?*

Unfortunately, it was years later before it occurred to me I simply was not allowing my "whole self" to show up and lead from the inside out. That, dear reader is exactly what this book will show you! While I knew business must go on and the show doesn't stop as you sort things out, intuitively I knew there had to be a better way. The big key is that this "better way" takes focused effort, support, tools, tips and limitless ongoing learning to forge through the daily grind of being an abundant business leader. The gift you are ultimately given, if you take the journey through this inspiring anthology, is powerful experiences that bring your personal values in line with your business objectives.

This anthology was created specifically to make your journey smoother and faster than some of us experienced; we shorten your journey as we share super successful business building strategies with a fresh approach... where being Abundantly You! starts from deep within. The intention of the anthology and the diverse messages included is to show others how to stand in their power as they seamlessly shift from the first entrepreneurial inspiration to being qualified to lead and run a business, become aligned with their values and beliefs, and engage in fruitful business actions. This knowledge and awareness is shared by hand-picked authors who offer valuable business concepts as dynamic and transformational business experts—each message leading you to a better place in what we call Abundantly You! On Purpose In Business.

50 Shades of Abundantly You! Marketing

Antoinette Sykes

People are in such a hurry to launch their product or business that they seldom look at marketing from a bird's eye view and they don't create a systematic plan.

~ Dave Ramsey (1982 -   )
American financial author, radio host, television personality, and motivational speaker.

It is of great pleasure that I share the one must-have business strategy at the core of your success... in being seen as an expert, a leader and simply authentic in your approach. That particular skillset I speak of is marketing. I believe marketing can be a divine tool to allow others to know of the fantastic offerings and solutions you provide. At the core of marketing lies your spirit and how you say what you say you do. Does marketing frighten you? If so, after assessing my approach and marketing options, it can be a piece of cake... as you show up more confident and true to your voice.

First, let's be very clear about what marketing is. Per Merriam-Webster, marketing is: *the total of activities involved in the transfer of goods from the producer or seller to the consumer or buyer, including advertising, shipping, storing, and selling.* The word *selling* intimidates a lot of business owners. If you fall in the trap of intimidation, just breathe deeply and read Dean's chapter, as a second "go to" on that topic. To be more concise, so you can anchor in the concept, marketing is the sum of all activities in which you engage to sell your goods or service.

When you think of marketing, consider having many conversations about your business offerings with your core values always infused in them. Understand, these conversations can take place online, via printed material, with the same tone as they would if you were sitting across a table... intimately chatting in person. Before going any further, identify your core values and/or your businesses core values. They are most likely similar if not the same. For example, one of my core values is integrity. Therefore every piece of my marketing communication is infused with truth and honesty, and always undergirded with integrity. That's also my personal core value. Follow? Once you identify your core values, your marketing decisions and conversations become a lot easier.

Next, accept marketing is also about persuasion, creative language and clever strategies to make your business-offering stand out from the rest.

Right now, think about some really memorable marketing you see on TV commercials or otherwise; what sticks out to you? What makes them catch your eye? Are they funny? Are they offensive? How many times did you see the commercial or promo before it really "stuck" with you? You owe it to yourself to stop and complete your list. The answers to these questions are key to you uncovering and applying some of the same tactics to your various marketing campaigns and overall daily marketing. The goal: always market consistently.

Once you've nailed down your core values and your approach, there are many ways to apply these factors to market your service or product offering. The below list is what I call 50 Shades of Abundantly You! Marketing.

Implementing a systematic marketing/business development approach in business is paramount. You will immediately see your dollars increase and your stress decrease as you experience less fear around marketing. Think of the following list as a secret weapon and always return to it when you need to move beyond your confort zone and vie for the next level.

Truth: when you are fearful, nothing but more fear follows. Let's grow your businesses in faith, by being Abundantly You! in your marketing.

How To Use

IN THREE EASY steps, you can begin to implement a new experience in marketing.

Review the list in its entirety—twice; follow up, making special note of all you currently implement in your business with a red check mark.

Review the list again; determine which you can immediately implement and highlight with a yellow marker.

Break out your calendar; write in 3-5 of the following "50 Shades of Marketing" you will implement this week.

By implementing 3-5 of these Abundantly You! Marketing Strategies, you will get more exposure and gain a peace of mind about where your next client or prospect is coming from.

1. Give away a sampling of your service.
2. Host a weekly themed luncheon or monthly party—low cost or no cost.
3. Ask five key clients for five referrals each.
4. Implement a referral system in your practice and make it generous and unique, and clearly communicate it to your clients.
5. Send a weekly or bi-weekly ezine.
6. Send out personalized thank you cards—for occasions and "just because!"
7. Write a special "juicy" report or ebook that is low cost or free.

8. Deliver excellence and value always—over deliver under promise.

9. Write an article around something new in your industry.

10. Know your vision; concisely communicate it with passion.

11. Make a daily impromptu call to a prospect — follow up and thank them for following you as you find out what's new in their business so you can be of service.

12. Socialize; attend an event once a week.

13. Post lead generation products and podcasts to relevant sites.

14. Update blog posts weekly or biweekly.

15. Post upcoming eventsand speaking engagements publicly on your website; send separately each week to the data list you maintain.

16. Identify the niche for your business where you can serve at your highest level and provide the greatest solutions to big problems.

17. Create compelling marketing scripts that win each time.

18. Complete regular offline and online mailings.

19. Make time for marketing each week; give the task priority, put it on your calendar and honor the commitment!

20. Break out of the box in your industry—do something different; be unique!

21. Make a list of organizations that need speakers and solicit them on a regular basis.

22. Hire and invest in a great business/marketing coach/mentor.
23. Pad your professionalism: what boards can you join to gain credibility and visibility?
24. Write a physical book or report or white paper (solo or anthology).
25. Create a one-sheet for marketing your skills as a speaker, workshop presenter, author, etc.
26. Host a tele-event.
27. Sponsor an event: organized races/walks, conferences and accompanying brochures, etc.
28. You are a problem solver—communicate that clearly.
29. Implement welcome sequences when new clients/prospects come into your sphere of influence that always give a "call to action" and spell out potential benefits.
30. Create a circle of support to remain in a positive frame of mind and forward motion.
31. Figure out your sweet spot for pricing.
32. Come up with a catchy tagline and/or URL (vanity url's).
33. Brand, brand, brand yourself and your business; each packs power when easily recognized.
34. Pen a column in a newspaper or relevant magazine.
35. Create attractive packages of products and services; make them easy to purchase.

36. Always give more value than the cost of your service or product—clearly communicate the value.
37. Host or launch a celebratory party for each new service offering, product or book.
38. Ask for the sale/business! If you don't ask, how will people know you are serious in your offering?
39. Create an operations plan/manual for easy implementation of your marketing activities into your regular business flow.
40. Offer varied pricing points; entry-level prices and products allow you to "funnel" customers to each successive product or service you provide. Rarely will anyone purchase your top-priced product until they have "tasted" one that comes with less risk and your credibility is established.
41. Ignore perfection; get marketing and product and service offerings out the door—course correct along the way.
42. Ask for feedback and use it to create new products, services or packaged offerings.
43. Have a rate sheet for client meetings; a menu of choices puts them in the place of being respected for the right to make decisions.
44. Speak your prospects language, not hard to understand verbiage.
45. Share your story to offer insight, empathy and more authenticity; when it is compelling you will find: Real Talk=Real Results.

46. Book interview spots with online and offline radio shows.

47. Screen and evaluate JV partnerships and take action on at least one a year. Make sure eachis a win/win proposition.

48. Coordinate direct mail campaigns at least once a quarter.

49. Frequently collect and post testimonials; calendar one block of time at minimum, quarterly.

50. Submit articles to third-party sites like: http://ezinearticles.com or http://sooperarticles.com

Looking For The Rewards

IT IS A given... no one wants to spend time on any activity that doesn't provide a positive result! Some people intuitively believe in the power of marketing; others either do not understand the benefits, the process or the return on investment. The ultimate benefit, if you like to think big, is to develop your entrepreneurial venture into a premier demand generation organization.

You can hope to lead a management staff that will utilize their combined experience to bring prospective clients superior customer care and positive profitable results, generated from the products and services you provide.

Although there are more reasons than financial gain when you seek to live life abundantly, the bottom line goal for most organizations is to increase revenue. My extensive industry experience and knowledge of demand generation allows staff to train, coach, motivate, monitor and act as a mentor for your business development. If you look at marketing from this perspective, you will take different actions.

Somehow, it just seems less burdensome, less expansive... when all you have to focus on is creating an "umbrella" of marketing programs that get customers deeply excited about your company's product and services. Thus, demand generation (marketing) programs help you reach new markets, promote new product and programs, build exciting consumer buzz, generate PR opportunities, and re-engage existing customers who may be feeling less inclined to look to you as the go-to person.

By understanding what you do and how you do it, your marketing activities become the extension of your organization that will get you in front of more "closable" opportunities.

Dig in! Embrace a new perspective of marketing and start growing your business.

About The Author

Transformation Life Coach, key anthologist, and publisher of the soon to debut *Faithpreneur Magazine,* Antoinette Sykes, is an integral key to others who seek to transform, transition and triumphantly live a quality of life they have previously only imagined—a life of freedom and unlimited happiness.

She serves up large portions of a fervent belief that you can live the life you truly dream of, yet never settle... if you trust all things are possible through the one that created you. As {An} Unsinkable Soul, Antoinette uses the knowledge derived from a BS in Psychology, MBA in Marketing, replete with the honored Subconscious Reconditioning Life Coaching certification. It no surpise to see Antoinette couple education with life experiences: as an elite workplace leader, survivor of two layoffs, and having lost her fiancé to suicide—to smilingly help others transform, transition and triumphantly live the life of freedom and unlimited happiness they've only imagined.

On any given day, Antoinette would tell her readers, "Today is the right day to make the right decision... ...to shift your mindset and move in a more positive, purpose-filled and productive direction!" Antoinette believes no one really has to look far.

10

The fire lies within and her passion is to help light that fire and incorporate concise steps to an upgraded edition of your vision for yourself and your life as an entrepreneur.

At any given time you can find Antoinette, who is a lover of life and all things self-help, living to her image of being ridiculously happy... inspiring the masses via speaking, social media or one of her coaching programs, and singing with her hairbrush as the microphone!

Contact:

http://standingtallrevolution.com/

antoinette@antoinettesykes.com

http://www.amazon.com/Antoinette-Sykes/e/B00CPRL0CS

https://twitter.com/AntoinetteSykes

Other Books by the Author:

Miracles, Momentum and Manifestation
http://www.amazon.com/dp/B00P2MZP5Q

Business Owner Tonight
http://www.amazon.com/dp/B00ATR25UW

{An} Unsinkable Soul
http://www.amazon.com/dp/0615952577

#BeSocial

Vida (Davida) Bratton

Facebook was not originally created to be a company. It was built to accomplish a social mission - to make the world more open and connected.

~ Mark Zukerberg (1984 -   )
American computer programmer and
Internet entrepreneur.

L aunching a business and working to be successful has not been an easy road. It has, however, been rewarding. One of the most gratifying revelations that has added value to my life, business, and ministry is the knowledge and understanding that we do live in a relational economy. And that will never change. Systems and tools may change, but never the fact that we must always know how to relate and connect. Stumbling on the power of Social media was an unforeseen blessing. Dedicated to living a life of purpose and encouraging and equipping others to do the same, I realized early on that mastering different Social media platforms would be of utmost importance.

These spaces allow me to be authentic, to add value in life and business and ultimately, to unapologetically live abundantly in my calling. And now it's time for you to do the same. It's time to #BeSocial.

Live In A Relational Economy

IT'S TIME TO #BeSocial. Yes! Be social. At the time of this writing, the world has approximately seven billion people and one-third of them utilize the Internet. Do you know what that means? It means you have access to the one-third who is on the web. While you ponder this, the steps necessary to close that gap of non-users are quickly approaching... with the higher utilization of a global partnership dedicated to making affordable Internet access available to the two thirds of the world not yet connected.

Wow! Does that not also indicate that sooner rather than later, the entire globe will be connected via the World Wide Web? How is that for targeted marketing? While our world is becoming more populated, it is becoming smaller. Why? For the first time in history people who live half-way around the world can now be connected with the click of a button. You are one like, follow, or friend away from your next connection, and Social Media has played the primary contributing role in leveraging the opportunity for the world to meet.

Facebook alone is the size of what could be the world's third largest country. It is also the leading Social Media platform, with Twitter running a far second. The topic of platforms is addressed later in more detail. There is an awesome infographic that was created by Emily Taing and Charlie Balk at Likeable.com; it offers great insight on the most popular platforms, the pro and cons, along with their best use.

The bottom line remains: Social Media is here to stay. Interwoven into the fabric of our countries, communities, homes, and businesses... myriad platforms are now the preferred way of connecting, learning, and yes—even conducting business. Are you prepared to utilize your social media platforms as a *lead generation* option?

How I Came To Be Social

I CAN REMEMBER feeling quite reluctant about using any social media platform. All I could think was, "That will be too many people all up in my business!" I also was extra careful and protective regarding my family, and still feel this way today as I practice activities to protect my family. Unfortunately, I was missing it... the real value and benefit of this type of viral marketing.

With most things in business development there is a learning curve. A part of which is deciding whether you really even **like** the tool you are using. Is it giving you what you want? Is it easy to maneuver? Can you connect the way you like to connect with people? And, the list goes on. And because I am one of those "over-achieving, do all things well" kind of people, I wanted to **master** my first platform: Facebook before considering another. Facebook was my introduction into the social media world, with Twitter and LinkedIn coming next, and in that order. I prayed, *let me do it right.* I would never post about my children and would be very selective with my pictures. But please know I was *looking* on everyone else's page! I was *lurking,* which is an essential tool I share later.

One day something happened. Right in the midst of my "refining process," what I like to call my Life Purpose Project, I found myself becoming more intrigued with how social media tools actually worked. While God was taking me through a process, He began to reveal more of what He needed me to do.

I became intrigued how it impacted my business while in the middle of launching my Life Purpose Project page, and wanted to learn as much as I could about effectively managing a Facebook page. I can remember saying to my husband, "I wonder if God is equipping us to teach others, such as the people in Marketplace Ministry and churches?" And we laughed at the very thought because at that time, my focus was on helping individuals find their purpose, and begin to fully "walk it out." I knew interacting with them daily via more than a post was going to be essential.

One day I woke up to a Groupon offer in my email... for Social Media Marketing University. I knew it could well be the key to rounding out what I had already learned about Social Media platforms.

I purchased the program and began to work through the curriculum; light bulbs began to illuminate my mind. I am not tech savvy by a long shot, but I had a great time working through these social media classes and also realized my natural knack for making and facilitating connections was coming alive through the very social media process I initially questioned! I began to connect with other businesses and people whom I could assist and who could assist me. The "Connection Queen" had begun her process... all while God graciously attached a skill hinged on connections to my DNA as a *Super Connector.* Not only was I going to be a relationship broker in person, I would now unlock the door to the masses on Social media... where countless connections are made daily.

Three Keys To Sizzling Social Media

THREE KEYS ARE essential to the success of any business or ministry leader who is responsible for building or maintaining a brand—whether a brick and mortar entity, a service-oriented, Internet business, church, ministry, or non-profit owner. If you are not a business owner, then this need not be your focus. However, if you are serious about reaching those God has called you to reach, touch, and facilitate transformation in their lives... keep reading and get ready to employ the KLD Method to put the sizzle into your social media!

Having Knowledge

The first key: Having Knowledge relative to the various platforms. Given that knowledge is power, ask yourself, "What do I know?" It is not possible to effectively utilize a tool without first understanding it. You need to know why a particular tool was created. What function does it have that other platforms do not? Does your target audience utilize this platform? The list of questions can become extensive, but the information can be acquired with relative ease utilizing Google searches and Infographics.

Additionally, you must know how to transform your efforts into results on each of the platforms you use. Engagement and conversion are the goals for business and ministry leaders alike. What that looks like will be different for each entity, but you must **know** the platforms you utilize. For example: if I am promoting a prayer call, the number of possible attendees via "likes" and "shares" is important to me. If I am hosting an event, it is important to know which posts cause people to visit my website or register.

Determine Your Preference

The second key is to determine which Social Media Platform you prefer and like working with. Once you learn the significance of each platform and how it can best help your business or ministry, then determine whether you even like the platform. While there are some things we do not like, but have to contend with, there are enough Social Media platforms that this need not become an issue. If you take the time to discover which one you prefer, you will utilize it more effectively. Do you like to give quick tidbits? Then you need Twitter. Do you like to create community? Then you need Facebook or Mightybell. Are you a do it yourselfer (DIY)? Then Pinterest is probably your home.

It is important that you "get" this, because ultimately, what you like drives what you accomplish, and there is a particular Platform (or more) for you that will feel right and comfortable.

It might also help you to know about my own preferences. I am not fond of LinkedIn, but I do like Instagram, which is also known as IG. The reason I like Instagram is because I am highly social. It also has a large audience of budding entrepreneurs who are innovative. Conversely, LinkedIn has a crowd that is corporate and older. While I am on LinkedIn and am comfortable with using it, I simply do not receive the same results. Thus, I don't like it as much. Similarly, you will begin to **like** the platforms you utilize and serve you well.

Do The Work!

The last of the three Keys, and perhaps the most important: you must Do what you know… on the platform you like. You may think this is a very simple concept, but far too many people neglect this essential piece. Do the work; it works! A simple, disciplined behavior—to acquire knowledge and apply it—works wonders in life, business and social media marketing. One reason this process is so effective is because social media is hot—people are always on—which makes it relevant, and current. Do you have a question you want answered? Post it. Are you not sure which outfit is best? Post it. Want to know which restaurant should you check out? Post it. Do the work on whatever platform you choose.

Sizzling Platforms

NOW, LET'S TALK about where you are going to do the work... engage and connect. While there are many, I will cover the five platforms I find most useful for business owners and ministry leaders: Facebook, Twitter, Instagram, Pinterest, and YouTube. You will learn the unique capabilities and effectiveness of each, utilizing the "know, like, and do strategies" just explained. A deeper awareness of each platform will make it easy for you to follow and apply the potential benefits to your business or ministry. A bonus platform—of which I have been a part of for over a year—will also be covered. This may be just what you need.

Facebook

Facebook is king! With that perspective in mind, it is a platform that best employs the "know, like, and do" method. There is no way around the reality that Facebook is the primary home for social media. There are many things to know, but the following three things you must *know* about Facebook.

There is no other marketing tool in the world for targeted marketing quite like Facebook. There is no other place to hone in so **closely on your niche.** Its Power Editor gives you more options to reach your audience than you ever thought possible.

Facebook offers several ways for you to **control the interaction with your audience.** Everyone has the privilege of creating a profile. And whether you are in business or an active ministry leader, you need a *Facebook Fan Page.* Another benefit is the ability to create *Facebook Groups.* The distinction: your basic Facebook profile is the standard page you get when registering with Facebook. The Fan Page is created more to conduct business, and comes with enhanced analytics that are hard to come by in other platforms. You can also utilize amazing advertising and promotion tools, scheduling tools, and more. Groups are small communities created around a certain topic or interest like weight loss, virtual yard sales and more. At this time you cannot advertise from groups. And thus is usually not the best option to engage with the masses.

Facebook provides you a totally **convenient process to interact** throughout Facebook Land by engaging on your profile or any fan page you manage. Most other social media platforms offer the inconvenience of requiring you log out and log back in as a different person/business.

There are two primary reasons why I normally **PREFER** Facebook to other social media options:

Touted as the **number one platform**, at the time of this writing, approximately one-third of the world uses it, with the remaining two-thirds slated to come on board within the next 10 years.

There is significant **value in tagging**. From your profile page, you can share any post you want with another person simply by using the tag feature at the bottom of a post. This is free strategy that allows you to quickly and easily "tag" by typing out a personal or business name in your post. If either is your "friend" or you "like" them, their name will populate as you type.

The exponential value: your more quickly gain exposure to a much wider reach than you would ever get by posting just to those who like or follow you. There is a thought in marketing about "going to the top of the apple tree" when you seek to serve a specific audience. Tagging allows you to do just that!

A vitally important consideration for Facebook is to create a Fan Page, and make the proper category selection at the time you complete the setup. Whether you are a business or a ministry, the correct option is to use a Fan Page rather than a personal one, which often proves to be totally ineffective.

With the right option, Facebook has built in systems to help you market successfully. Since your profile reaches those with whom you have some connection, share it! Your profile will be relatively ineffective if you are constantly trying to reach viewers in "another pond!"

Twitter

Twitter is considered the second largest social media platform, and known as the home of "micro-blogging." If you have thoughts that are pertinent to your business or ministry and want to disperse them over time, Twitter is for you! The unique feature of Twitter is the offer of almost constant conversation. To take the greatest advantage of this platform, the following elements are a "must know."

Twitter is a micro blog, which by definition, is a web service that allows subscribers to broadcast short messages to each other.

You are allowed **140 characters or less per post**. I note "or less" because if you want to tag someone, add a picture, or hashtags, then your character count is reduced to accommodate.

Query searches on Twitter using hashtags are one of the best ways to find relevant conversations you can join. Using your hashtag and searching for other hashtags relevant to your topic are how connections are made on Twitter.

Re-tweeting is your friend! It is one of the best tools to **connect with like-minded brand owners**

and individuals. Re-tweeting shows your interest in a topic and support for another Twitter user.

What I really **LIKE** about Twitter is:

The ripeness of Twitter's platform for followers is great! Because the exchange (Tweets) is so short, **people respond quickly.** And there is always a thread about breaking news on Twitter. When Pharrell's "Smokey the Bear' hat hit the stage at the Grammy's, a Twitter account was immediately created for it; at the time of this writing, it currently has 19.6k followers.

The day I received the most followers, I had participated in a class and we were instructed to use certain hashtags. My alerts were dinging through the night. It was a wonderful feeling.

I like the ability to **create *lists* on twitter.** This tool allows you to interact with your followers in groups based on categories you create. It is remarkable because it helps you **to separate the people you follow** and search what is happening under the list you create. In terms of efficiency, this is sometimes much better than viewing all of the people you follow at one time, which, if you think about it, can be quite overwhelming.

One thing you **HAVE TO DO** on Twitter is participate in Twitter Chats, which are great.

They will "ease" you into Twitterville, with the result of meeting new people and making fast friends. The topics are endless; the chats are scheduled on a regular basis. Take a few moments and visit the following "schedule of Twitter chats:

http://www.vidabratton.com/BeSocial/

Just "hop in and have fun!"

Instagram

Instagram, also known as IG, is yet another "happening" platform right now. Especially for millennials, or those who want to reach and audience filled with the Millennial Generation or Generation Y. This platform currently appeals to affluent teens and young adults, with Twitter holding a fast second, and Facebook trailing in third place. Even though the millennials are the core focus, Instagram still holds significant value for all brands, businesses, and ministries. If you are called to reach the millennials, look no further.

What you must KNOW about Instagram is:

At the time of this writing, you can **only upload photos to Instagram using your smartphone**. However, you can view your account and other accounts from a tablet or computer. You can also "like" photos from your tablet or laptop. There are currently developers creating tools that will allow higher-level functions from your computer, but there is currently not much buzz about it.

Instagram is for **pictures or 15-second videos only**. You can only write or type after you have uploaded one of these two. Your writing is placed in the comment section of the picture. It does take some getting used to at first because it is a completely different way of interacting. I must say, that once you have gotten familiar with this platform, you will **love** it.

Hashtags rule in IG Land. And knowing which hashtags rule is half the battle. You can find a list of top 25 IG hashtags at:

http://vidabratton.com/besocial/

These are terms most searched and followed on IG. If you want to be discovered, gather your hashtags and get moving.

There is so much to like about IG; the two things I LIKE are:

It is a **picture information platform**. For the first time it is possible to be visually stimulated while receiving information, providing a picture of what the person is sharing with words for explanation. The only down side is there are no hyperlinks in the written post. Hyperlinks are only in the bios of each user.

I also like Instagram's **tagging capabilities**. You can tag someone you follow even if they do not follow you. This is a powerful way to get your post and picture to people whom you want to see it.

The one thing you must DO on Instagram is:

Hashtag. I know this sounds redundant, but this is how people find you. You have to remember...

on IG you are viewing one long stream of pictures and info. But the explore page gives the option to search users or hashtags. And because people don't use their names all the time, if their hashtag is known, or their brand, you find them doing the hashtag search. It's a powerful tool!

Pinterest

I love Pinterest! Like most Social Media platforms, the key is getting used to its unique features and knowing how it operates. Again, as your brand, business or ministry develops, you will be intuitively drawn to the platform you need. Pinterest is interesting because it is the only platform that offers a wholistic view of your brand to the world.

According to *Business Insider*, between the fall of Fall-2013 and Spring-2014, the percentage of 18 to 29 year-olds using Pinterest rose from 25% to 33%, which represented a greater adoption increase than that of Snapchat—the number one platform for teenagers.

You must KNOW these three things about Pinterest.

> This story board platform caters to all demographics and is popular amongst the **wealthiest consumers**. This is good information, especially if your product caters to a wealthier clientele. It's important to know where to find them.70% of women are on Pinterest. Can you believe that? This is more than any other Social Media platform. And most of them are there on Saturday mornings! What a **great platform to**

reach women if they are a part of your niche. This is a great time to interact with brands and repin from others.

Pinterest just implemented advertisement **options for business accounts.** This additional service is slated to give Pinterest a competitive edge with other platforms.

What I LIKE about Pinterest is:

The option of creating **a board for every idea** that I have. Coupled with the option of changing the covers of the board, this can be a **great lead-generating tool.** When you are running a special or have a big announcement, creating a board is essential and powerful! Then adding pictures that capture the essence is a plus. It also gives your clients a well-rounded view of who you are. Clients love to connect among those with whom they do business.

Re-pinning from websites to your Pinterest board is easily functioned. If you are reading a blog or article and the site has Pinterest enabled, you can 'pin' directly to your board. This is total convenience and saves time.

What you must DO on Pinterest is:

Create your boards and 'Like' other pinner's pictures and follow their boards. That's it. Pinterest is the most **fun and interactive platform,** with the least amount of work. But be careful. You can get drawn into the abyss, and be there for a while.

YouTube

YouTube is a truly interesting platform because it combines video with Social Media. It allows people to connect with the person who posts the video. When a person posts a video they post to their 'channel,' which is promoted for subscriptions. And similar to a blog, when the owner of a YouTube channel posts something new, subscribers get the video. People have done some fabulous things with YouTube, like starting talk shows, doing reviews and creating tutorials. If you don't know how to do something… go to YouTube. If you want to see something that has been viewed at all on television or the web… go to YouTube.

I only have one important thing to **KNOW** about YouTube.

YouTube is the 2nd **largest search engine on the Internet.** This means that you will be among the second largest search engine on the web with your product or brand. Coupled with other Social Media business builders, you can drive people straight to your channel. This is great for those of you who would rather create exciting videos than write a blog, although a combination is best.

What I **LIKE** about YouTube is:

You can **start your very own channel**. You can dedicate it to your cause and talk about it. Coupled with the fact that videos get higher conversion, v-logging (video blogging) is a great idea for any brand owner. People can see your face and connect with you visually. And, since people can comment on your videos, you expand visibility any time you inspire dialogue.

You can **create more than one channel.** I see many brand owners do this when their focus shifts. One may start out in network marketing and use their channel to talk about their business. Then after successfully working with that company for a while, they create another channel that is geared toward training and not necessarily product information. It allows you to expand your visual brand and separate topics, creating less confusion for viewers.

What you have to DO on YouTube:

Create a channel and start v-logging. Even if your posts are less than a minute long, that's perfect; in fact, the shorter... the better. This idea is pretty consistent across social media platforms, too. You don't want to overwhelm viewers with anything exceedingly long. Play it smart! Mix your messages up a little by creating some that are longer than others. Note: Uploading videos to YouTube is a breeze; it is fast and easy. One of the easiest ways to accomplish the task is to use your smartphone or tablet. Record right into YouTube and Voila! You're done. You can then take that link and post it to other Social Media Platforms.

Bonus Platform: MightyBell

MIGHTYBELL IS A brand new platform created by developers who worked with other Social Media companies like Twitter. They wanted to create a place where people could establish and maintain a smart, professional community with a purpose. The only other Social Media platforms that are remotely close to accomplishing this are Facebook Groups and Meetup.

But Mighty Bell has really given thought to the platform that allows you to create "Communities" and then add "Circles" to your communities. This has now leveraged opportunities for leaders to create a national brand and then create sub communities, based on myriad things: gender, location, age, and experience, all within a larger community. If you have a brand, business, or ministry that will reach beyond your local market, check out this platform. It can serve as your gathering place to stay connected and an extension of your website.

MightyBell is unique and like no other platform because their team will work with you to establish viable communities utilizing the unique features of the platform. They will help establish the best stage for your particular niche. And an added bonus is having the option to use your unique web address. Like Meetup, there are fees associated after reaching a certain number of members. But, depending on your goals it's *totally* worth it. I encourage you to spend some time reviewing the MightyBell website at: mightybell.com.

Keys To Connections

ALL THE INFORMATION presented is purposeful to learn and navigate Social media platforms. These tips help you promote and connect. Please remember that connections are vitally important. The platform God has called you to create, while you lead, cannot be accomplished alone. Connections are key! And Social Media is highly effective if you choose to #BeSocial.

Utilize the following three tips on connecting;

Connect your product or brand with the most unique, best possible consumer. If you have a brand and no one knows about it, you don't have a brand. Wise marketing is the foundation to best utilizing Social Media. If you are not currently using social media platforms for business, push your brand out slowly. If you have been using these tools *effectively*, take it up a notch.

Reach out to other business and ministry *leaders* and engage in mutually beneficial *Joint Ventures;* sometimes referred to as JV events. Joint Ventures require taking the best of both leaders to combine forces and provide amazing events for a shared client base. If you are unfamiliar with the term, Joint Venture... Google it.

Smart marketing calls for **creating #Hashtags that signify your brand** and using them consistently. If you were to "Google" my alias #ConnectionQueen, you would see many pictures and platforms that, for the most part, refer back to me. Hashtags are used to find you, your brand, and products. It's one of the most amazing tools ever created. Why? Because they pull your information together... in one location. For example, if you were to search "connection," a list of items referring to connections would come up; however, when your search-term is #connectionqueen you will find a list *specifically* about Vida Bratton and my brand. The hashtags are placed on posts and pictures you create; and always send people back to your primary sites, via your hashtags.

Remember! #BeSocial

THE MOST IMPORTANT point to remember is that you have to #BeSocial. If you are not going to reach out and target your niche in the marketplace, then you may be opting for an unnecessrily long road to success. Some believe Social Media is a waste of time and not effective. I most ardently disagree! These are usually the thoughts of individuals who have yet to learn how to use the platforms correctly.

If managing your Social Media platforms is not your forte, don't do it! Find someone who can best accomplish the task for you. You can view a social media manager-hiring checklist on my website. If you are just beginning to invest in this type of marketing, a good Social Media Plan is important. Such a plan offers brand owners direction and action steps that guide and help them to remain consistent. Take into consideration your comfort level, type of brand or platform, and your goals.

Being social is but one aspect of fully being Abundantly you! It is also just one small part of building a business on purpose. It is, however one of the most important decisions you can make for your ministry or business to #BeSocial. As you will have discovered throughout my chapter, it is necessary to open your heart and mind and begin thinking far beyond your local sphere of influence. When you are grounded and passionate about the messages you are to purposefully deliver in this world, you can then embrace the reality that there are people waiting to hear your voice in the world. Your ministry or business is an answered prayer to someone across the country or perhaps on the other side of the world. Take the challenge; employ the KDL (Know, do and like) model, and the three steps to connecting today... and then go to work!

About The Author

Co-founder of the **Life Purpose Project** and **The Life Centre** with her husband, Ty Bratton, this energy driven, gifted and talented woman is committed to encouraging, equipping, and empowering others to walk in their God-Purpose. She lives out her God-Purpose, as she lovingly co-labors in ministry with her husband, speaks in the marketplace, and trains leaders to *Develop Wings, Take Leaps of Faith, and Soar!*

Vida believes when the right energy is directed toward destiny, greatness is the only possible result. A Minister, Relationship Broker, Social Media and Business Strategist, and Super Connector, she is affectionately known as the Connection Queen.

Vida awakes each day... ready to accept her next opportunity to partner with business and ministry leaders who are ready to #BeSocial and activate #StilettoFaith. She is excited about her newest endeavor "Virtuous Womanpreneur."

Vida Bratton received her BA in Sociology and African and African-American Studies from the University of Virginia. She holds an M.A. degree from New York University in Higher Education Administration. Vida has over 15 years of the service areas of: Ministry, K-12 Education, Higher Education, Social Services, Non-profit Leadership, community connections, and Entrepreneurship. She counts it a blessing to currently serve on the Board of Directors for the World Wide Women Group, Inc.

Contract:
www.vidabratton.com
info@vidabratton.com

Starting A New Business

Start-up Anxiety, Supportive Relationships and Business Income Growth Strategies

Anna Long

Be yourself; everyone else is already taken
~ Oscar Wilde (1854-1900)
Irish writer and poet.

S uccess in business begins from somewhere deep within; it takes awareness, effort, tools and tips to forge a pathway to success. Starting a New Business helps readers to stand in their power and, in becoming aligned with business values and action.

My Story

WHILE I CAN'T technically say that I came out of my mothers' womb an entrepreneur, this statement isn't far off from the truth. There is a certain creative magic that comes from bringing a new business to life and I've had the entrepreneurial itch for years.

Other than the creative abundance that starting and growing a business affords, I find it freeing to have the control to set something up for myself that can make as much or as little money as I want.

Because while I can't control what people pay me, I can control what rates I set and how many hours I work (take that job!)

Money has always fascinated me. Despite having chosen to get my Master's Degree in Social Work, which has proven to be not the most lucrative of my career choices, I have always loved money and the feeling of freedom that came with having it!

When I was young I always wanted to be older so that I could partake in this miraculous "workplace exchange" where people would pay me to do things that, as a child, I had to do for free... like cook, clean, be nice to people, etc. My pre-adolescent years were sprinkled with penny-producing ventures such as selling rocks on the side of our gravel driveway, hosting garage sales and cleaning my grandpa's house each week for $14.00... just so I could get my hands on new CD's.

Shortly after my 15th birthday I got my very first job and became addicted to saving my earnings. I didn't know what I was saving for, but I was pretty sure it would involve a plane ticket out of Idaho so that I could see more of what the big world had to offer. In fact I was pretty sure I would be doing amazing stuff in my life—I just had no idea what I wanted to do—well, other than leave Idaho of course!

I worked a handful of jobs in high school that included restaurant hostess, pizza delivery driver and eventually, after begging long and hard, my first job as a waitress at Perkins. If you've never heard of

Perkins, they are sort of like Denny's; just with better baked goods. *Don't be mad Denny's—you still get the vote for most creative menu-naming strategies.* Oh! The life lessons that were provided as I learned to multi-task like a mad-woman, wear a smile when I was screaming inside, and make some serious plate artwork with raspberry dessert syrup.

I spent the next eight years getting degrees, and working in non-profits from Seattle-to-Chicago-to-Portland. I learned I was discontented staying in one place or one job for too long. I discovered working a set 9-5 schedule felt like prison and that my biggest dreams were beyond those that society had set for me. I also found I was happier if I ask, "How can I make more money ?" rather than, "How can I cut back?"

Somewhere in the mix of it all I went to school nights and weekends to become an esthetician (skin care lady) and fumbled my way into creating my first "for real" business.

Face Fear And Overcome Challenges

IF YOU'VE EVER started your own business, you've probably come face to face with your fear. I've found that growing a business challenged me to grow more as a person than anything else I've done in my life. I've never had to face my fears head-on in quite the same way or at quite the same rate as I have in being a business owner.

Do you have a hard time talking yourself up? Get over it!

Do you hate public speaking? Too bad!

Feel fat on camera? Sorry, get on with it!

That's right, any fear you have, even if you didn't know you had it, will surface and fester when you become an entrepreneur. But that's ok, that's the main reason that we **grow** so much on our way to success!

So what were my blocks?

It might be easier to start with what were not my blocks? I had so many obstructions when I first started my business that no one but my best friends even knew about them. I was afraid:

I wasn't good enough, or my treatment room wasn't nice enough...

To market myself or my business because I was afraid that people would think I had a huge ego...

To ask people to pay me for my facials and energy work because I was afraid that they didn't have enough money to pay me.

Do you see the theme here?

I clearly had a ton of fear and it continually surfaced because I had blocks around promoting myself, making money and owning my value.

In a world where my competition was charging $90-$135 an hour for a facial... I was charging $45. In a world where most estheticians were giving heartless facials with the sole purpose of selling customers creams they didn't need, I gave a piece of my spirit to each client and refused to even ask for a sale.

I clearly struggled to find the middle ground in creating a successful business that encompassed my values, but also allowed me to profit at the level I deserved. Eventually I **did** create a successful skincare practice, which I eventually sold to create the time and space to pursue my desired business strategy—my current business named the *Electric Empire.*

Before sharing my tips to growing a profitable business, it's important for you to take a minute and consider your own blocks. I know that it can be painful to come face to face with your fears, but you certainly can't work through them if you don't first identify what they are. So take a moment and reflect.

What blocks currently hold you back from creating or growing your business?

Secret: Create A Profitable Business

FIRST AND FOREMOST, I want to mention that just because you have a profitable business, it doesn't mean that it is automatically a happily abundant one! It is possible to make a lot of money and not be happy with the way you have set up your business. I'll write more about this later.

Secondly, it is possible to feel abundant in your business without making money; however if you want a business, and not simply another hobby, it will be crucial to move you into a profitable position as soon as possible. If you aren't making money yet, don't feel badly—we all have to start somewhere.

A profitable business can look like a lot of different things to different people. To some it may look like making millions and to others it may mean making just enough to replace your day job.

After years of growing my own businesses and helping countless others grow theirs, I discoverer there are 10 main fundamental components that all truly profitable business owners tend to use effectively.

It's my hope that by sharing these elements, you will have a good idea of what you need to work towards as you start a new business. If you already have a business and are struggling with being profitable, it is my hope that this list will provide you with a few good ideas on which to re-focus your energy and efforts.

Have A Well-defined Business Idea

THIS MAY SEEM like a no-brainer but you'd be surprised at how many businesses fail because they simply aren't clear about the business they want to create. Look at your business idea as a starting point for any current or future endeavors, where you begin a new life... that of a business and your own life as an entrepreneur.

I recommend you dig deeper into the benefits you provide to your clients—or plan to provide to them—and position your business around them.

When I talk about "benefits" I'm not talking about features.

When you buy a Mercedes, the *features* might include things like leather seats, sunroof, etc. But *benefits,* on the other hand, might include things like feeling wealthy, making other drivers envious, etc. You may not think any of these things are benefits, but the people who buy these cars don't typically buy them simply because they are good cars; they buy them because there is a certain identity associated with them. The creators and marketers behind the Mercedes brand fully understand the dynamics.

What are the true benefits of what you do?
~ Anna Long

Define And Claim Your Uniqueness

YOU MAY HAVE better skills, more integrity, and even more attractive body parts, than your competition, but if you can't define what makes you uniquely awesome, and market it, then no one will know! And if they don't know, they won't buy.

I recommend you do whatever you must to figure out how you are unique—both in life and in business. This could require searching your soul, asking clients, or even hitting up friends to get a more objective perspective about why you are unique.

When I first started my consulting business I sent out an email survey to my friends and family so I could get a better idea about the personality traits

43

and attributes they admired in me. This gave me a jump start to better understand how I was different than other business consultants.

Another thing that will help you differentiate yourself is to thoroughly understand your competition. If you are just forming a business idea, you may not be sure who your competitors are, and that's ok. You can always come back to this exercise later when you have a better idea of what you provide.

The trick to research your competition is that you can't let it get you down! There are great people in every industry and **you** can be one of them. There can be, and usually is, more than one great business in your industry. Embrace your competition and understand what makes them tick. When you have a better grasp on who they are and what they provide, you can focus on yourself and have a better appreciation of the unique skills and traits that set you apart. Alternatively, you can also use this exercise to decide what is lacking in the services provided by your competition—and make that lacking element precisely what it is you will provide!

Know Who You Want To Work With

IT IS ESSENTIAL you understand the dynamics of the relationships you will have with people you will want to work with, and those you don't; working with *just anyone* is a sure-fire recipe for burn-out and failure. I know it's tempting when you first start a business to work with anyone who is willing to have you serve them. After all, money is money, right? Wrong! There are clients who make your work seem like magic and there are others who will make you want to throw in the towel and give up. The work is exactly the same, it's the energetic struggle that can drain you when you take on clients that aren't a good fit. I call these good clients "ideal clients" and I'm always on the lookout for them!

I recommend if you already have clients or customers to make a "do like" and "don't like" list and assess the experiences you have had. The process is easy and will give you a headstart to begin marketing to the quality of clients you want versus those you know intuitively you don't. The more clearly your marketing messages represent *who* you do choose to support, the more easily your message is heard and responded to by those *ideal clients!* If you don't have a business yet, evaluate the personality traits of friends, family, and co-workers who drive you crazy (in good **and** bad ways). This is another exercise to determine who you want to work with and who you want to avoid!

When you have this list front and center in your mind—even if you don't share it openly— you will be shocked to see how things will begin to shift for you. I do this once or twice a year as new issues come up and I'm often shocked at how simply creating this list seems to help attract ideal clients and keep the rotten ones away. You will also find paying attention to this list helps you create both messages and policies and procedures that "head off" the potential problems!

Tell A Story People Want To Hear

BY AND LARGE, you will find people don't connect with businesses; they connect with inspiring, trustworthy people. So being able to share your story, through the written word and copy, Is invaluable to the growth of your business.

I recommend you are strategic in crafting the About Page on your website. It is one of the most visited pages on a website, especially if you are referring people to it whom you've met at networking events; people always want to know about **you**.

When you put extra effort into creating an about page and a brand story that are appealing and speak to your skills—and are congruent with the needs and wants of your ideal clients, magic happens and "selling" is no longer as much work!

Start by picking a few prominent stories about your life, how you do business, the people you have served, etc. Tease out the themes, and figure out what's most valuable to reveal to people who visit your site. You have one time to make a good first impression, which in today's technology is often your website.

You may be interested in knowing for me this process took at least a month. I wrote about 11 pages about me and how I got to where I am today. Because the "path" can sometimes be a bit messy, if you are not able to get in sync with the "theme" you want to promote, readers have a tendency to do nothing more than "get lost" in a massive collection of "words." Clear, complete and concise works every time; write as though you were pouring your heart out to your readers, and then refine your copy until you have a succinct message that defines, leads, and compels!

After I wrote those 11 pages I went through and highlighted the themes that seemed to really define me—transition, curiosity, love for business, etc.. I then picked a few key stories that to this day, clearly and succinctly make up a compellling background of my brand story.

Not only did this process help me write better copy for my about page, it helped me to easily and concisely describe how I serve others.

Services, Courses, And Products

ONCE YOU CREATE your business, you need to be clear in how you offer and package it, and understand how to price yourself to be correctly positioned in the market that best represents your offering.

I recommend that when you sell "stuff" you learn it can be easier to sell without over-thinking the process. When you sell yourself or services, it takes more effort to package what you offer so that potential clients can purchase from you.

For instance, when I first became a business strategy consultant I didn't simply say, "Hey, book me if you want a strategy." No, instead I created a specific service around a particular problem I recognized a lot of business owners struggled with, which happened to be uncovering their most unique skills and creating an offer around how they could use those skills to best serve others.

My first offer was called the "Special Sauce Session" and I booked 10 people who were having a difficult time understanding how they stood out in their market. I completed research and intuition-based counseling to uncover what I saw as their *diamond assets.*

To discover and implement a very clear and specific service is what allowed me to kick off my consulting business without having to create a custom package for each business owner. It also allowed me to be very specific in my target marketing, which is always easier; the process also helped me better understand my own skills.

Generate Compelling Website Copy

BEFORE I STARTED my business, I had no idea what the term "copy" meant. Now I live and breathe it! Copy includes the words on your website or your marketing materials. Until you can describe your services in way that connects and convinces your prospective clients, your results will be nothing much more than heading down the *preverbial creek without a paddle.* Without good copy you are relying on "luck" to turn website traffic into the wealth you want. And luck is most certainly not a business plan!

I recommend you start by writing a great About Page that encompasses your story, your client's primary struggle or problem, and how you strive to benefit them with the solutions you can provide. Then move on to writing your other website copy such as Work with me, your Homepage, etc.

Whether you are an independent business owner or you have a big company, your brand should have an identifiable "voice." Developing your voice can take some practice, but the best way to get good at this is to write… and write often.

If you have some concern you are terrible at writing and the process holds you back, then consider hiring a copywriter. They may end up saving you a ton of time, and help you make more money, more quickly.

Set Up A Website Geared To Success

IF YOU ARE just starting out and don't have the budget to hire a killer designer—although you should eventually—then you will have to build your own website.

I recommend you create a WordPress website, use an easy drag and drop theme like Elegant Theme's Divi Theme, and get professional photos taken sooner rather than later. This mix of do-it-yourself and professional approach will give your site a good appearance while you work on showcasing your new business!

Market Strengths And Weaknesses

WE ALL HAVE certain blocks that prevent us from stellar marketing. You need to *get over them* so you can be comfortable marketing your services, courses, or products. You also need to learn how to *play to your strengths* when you do market.

I recommend you figure out just where your "marketing blocks" came from. Is there a story around marketing that you tell yourself that prevents you from speaking up about what you do? If you can trace back where your story originated, you can ultimately face it and move beyond it.

Also get very real about what you are **naturally good** at. Are you good at chatting with people face to face or are you better at making friends in the online world? Choose one main way to market (online or offline) based on what you are naturally good at and get your first set of clients this way! When you show up consistently authentic, the know, like and trust factors people need are developed organically and far more quickly.

Save Time And Money: Use Systems

GET YOUR CONTRACTS, payment methods, email, and booking systems in order when you are less busy; set yourself to best manage success when you do get busy!

I recommend you pick one "system" each week you want to tackle, and research how you can improve it. For instance, if you want clients to be able to easily pay for your services or goods online, then you need to research the best ways to accept payment—pick one and then set it up! No dragging your feet, it will only cause you and your current or future clients more hassle than needed! Then, the following week, pick another... until all your systems are set up and running smoothly.

And last but not least...

Sell Without Feeling Sleazy

SELLING DOESN'T HAVE to make your stomach turn! Selling should feel easy, natural and even fun.

I recommend: Shifting your sales mindset. Sales is never about "convincing someone to buy." Instead, it's about inviting people, who need what you sell, to buy the very thing that will help them improve their lives. I also recommend giving freely when you are starting out to gain experience and momentum!

I know this extensive list might seem loomingly large... and quite scary, but when you break it down into executable steps and consistently move through them, you will make serious progress towards launching and profiting from your new business.

I also know that these ten recommendations may seen like a lot, but when you break them down into

51

definite steps and you consistently move through them, you will recognize success in the most uncommon hours; finding you are abundantly you! and on purpose in business. I believe in you! Let's do this!

About The Author

Anna Long is a spark plug, the savvy, and yes, intuitive business strategist behind Electric Empire, where she's helped hundreds of women turn their ideas and talents into highly purposeful and successful businesses.

Her business came to fruition because she held tight to one core belief: *You must live from your higher purpose in order experience all that life has to offer you.* Equipped with a Master's Degree in Social Work and a passionate belief women play an integral part in being "of service" in the world, Anna leads women to access their intuition... in insightul and powerful ways. It is embuing others with the sense of using this power to make the world a more positive place that Anna finds the life she desires, and inspires others to do the same.

When she's not cheerleading or strategizing her clients' successes, you can find her traveling the world with her husband Shea.

Contract:
www.electric-empire.com
http://electric-empire.com/dreamers-revolution/
info@electric-empire.com

Put Your Name On It

Lessons To Create Abundant Change In Life and Business

Shari Molchan

Fortune favors the brave.

~ Latin Proverb

T he following is a series of stories that ultimately deliver a series of lessons I've learned and earned on my journey to financial freedom and success. Sometimes, you have to look back on your past to decide what shifts will create an Abundantly You! If you've arrived at the pivotal moment of having decided to create your own financial freedom and abundance, this message and these lessons are for you. Go out and get it!

My Money Roots

I'M EIGHTEEN YEARS old and about to get married. It's 1980. I met my future husband exactly six months ago, seven months before I graduated from high school. This isn't what I imagined as a young girl—What? No white-knight whisking away the princess! I went to a small town for a weekend with a friend and ended up not leaving, and now, I'm about to say, "I do." Except he never asked me to marry him, not the bend down on your knee fantasy that every girl craves. So how did I get here?

When I shocked everyone by moving in with him after spending a weekend, the family pressure was on, and the questions flew.

"What are you doing?"

"Do you love him?"

I didn't know. I was running away from a dysfunctional family filled with divorces and insecurity that accompanies life with stepparents... I just knew I was confused.

I know now I was looking for stability and love. Being far away from all of the angst of my current family felt like a good place to start. So I left friends and family to move to this small town, where I knew no one.

I was playing house, playing the wife—I didn't have much of a role model to follow (I'll write about that later). He was ten years older than me and owned a large lot with a trailer on it. I thought, *I have stability, financially anyway. Maybe the love will come soon. I hope.*

Three months rolled into four; the pressure started up again from my family.

"Get a commitment from him."

"If you are going to live with him, then you should get married."

So we did. He never asked me to marry him; I didn't get an engagement ring. It was more like, "Okay, well, let's do it." And our parents started planning.

Oh, yes, I got the white dress, and family members organized a potluck reception in the local hall. But for me it was more like a party with friends than a wedding. *I am married—really?*

To this day I still cannot recall my feelings; I had buried who I was so deeply it would take another twenty years for me to realize it, but that, too, comes later.

He was in control of all the money and ran the house. I don't even remember how or when he gave me money for things like groceries, but he must have. I got a job in the local grocery store to earn some spending money and enjoyed that very much, but I had no real connection with money or finances.

We ended up building a house on the one-half acre lot the trailer was on; he continued managing the money and bills. We had a joint checking account, and he had me write in an accounting journal every penny spent and where it went. He was a very aggressive man with a short temper, and I dared not cross him.

Two years later, my first son was born. I'd never had a burning desire to have kids like some women do, but when I held him in my arms; I fell in love, and found the connection I had so long craved for so long. *Am I finally recognizing my need for family, something unmet from my parents' divorces?* My biological father had left and remarried when I was two, and a new father adopted us. This relationship also ended in divorce when I was just eight years old.

Two-and a half years after I had my first, my second son was born.

Although I loved my boys, my husband's anger and agression wore me down. In our marriage, if that's what you want to call it, I never once felt connected with or loved by him. Without healthy relationship role models, I had no idea what that should even look like. Eventually, when my youngest son was one and a half years old, my husband crossed the line and physically assaulted me in a drunken stupor; divorce number one became inevitable.

Assault is the tipping point for me to leave. But where do I go and how will that work?

I had never lived on my own or taken care of the finances by myself like a grownup. The first of many moments of reality hit me—if I wanted to go anywhere, I had to get a car, and I couldn't qualify on my own. My ex would have to co-sign.

Big Waves Of Lessons

LIFE COMES AT us, sometimes in soft, undulating waves of comfort; sometimes with a force so powerful there's no way you can fail to recognize the

Put Your Name On It!

lesson it intends to teach. The vehicle purchase brought Lesson #1 to me: Know what you're signing up for. Because I didn't fully evaluate what I was buying, the car salesman sold me a lemon, which would later cost me thousands of extra dollars.

Next up in grownup finance management, I needed a credit card. When I went to the bank to apply for one, I was told I didn't have a credit rating and therefore could not receive a card. What? I had owned a house, we had credit cards, and I was in that marriage for four years. How can that be?

The tidal wave of Lesson #2 swept over me: **Put your name on it**. I subsequently learned my name was not on the title of anything owned during our marriage, not the house or the credit card. Oh, yes, I'd had a credit card, but it was just a second card with the credit in his name only.

Some waves are so strong, and sweep so high, they take your breath away. Such was Lesson #3: **Don't put your head in the sand about money, and get the help you need**. For instance, if you're in the midst of a divorce, secure a lawyer to get what's fair. When I left the marriage, I primarily focused on leaving with my emotions intact. Only much later I discovered I was also entitled to his pension for the five years I took care of our kids and did not work outside the home. When he told me I couldn't afford the mortgage payment, I foolishly bought into his *offer* to keep the house and the debt, totally unaware there was over $100,000 equity that I would never see, but to which I was entitled.

59

Instead, I found myself at twenty-four years of age, with two children under the age of five, totally at the mercy of family and friends to help me out. I moved into an affordable town house, but quickly realized that I had not budgeted enough money to pay all the bills and still buy groceries for my children.

Budget? I didn't even know what that word meant!

Not to mention I hadn't found a job yet. At the encouragement of friends who said I would qualify, I applied for welfare. I was grateful for the six months' assistance available to me until I secured a new job. This entire life transition was very humbling, and definitely not how I had envisioned my picture perfect life.

For all the ways I found my life being disrupted and disappointing, I found myriad others in which life did show me favor. I was fortunate to get a job at a major grocery store at a starting salary of $12.00 per hour. I made fairly good money, based on the salary levels in the late 80's. Also, my brother's friend, a loan officer at a local credit union, not only got me started with a credit card to build my credit rating, but also helped me secure a personal loan to pay off the one that still had my ex-husband's name on it. *Now, tell me again... why did I have to pay for his debt and have nothing to show for it in the end?*

Let me tell you, I felt so empowered. I felt like a big girl—financially—for the first time. I remember the day I went into the bank that held the loan with my ex's name on it. It was the same bank that had denied me a credit card. When I went up to the teller and said that I wanted to give them the cashier's check to pay off my loan, well, now the bank finally decided to pay attention to me.

The teller wanted me to wait and talk to the loan manager about the loan! I waited for far too long, and finally said, "Here, just take the check; I have to leave."

As I was leaving, the manger literally chased me and called me to come back and talk.

I replied, "Thanks for nothing. Oh, and I will never be back." To this day I have maintained my sense of empowerment by not having to deal with that bank.

The event was not without the ripples of Lesson #4: **Don't settle for what someone tells you**. When you want something to happen in your best interest, don't just settle for the first answer you get. There is another bank or service that will work for you. The point is, service companies should be working *for* you, not the other way around. Also, learn to live within the reality that banks in general are not your friends; their #1 concern is the bank's interest, not yours.

To have the maximum privilege in financial matters, you need to first have a healthy relationship both with your money and the bank so that you retain some control over your life, and your finances. That control comes with gaining basic financial knowledge about credit, debt, etc. Unfortunately, at that point I had neither a relationship with, nor knowledge or control of finances. But I was certainly open to learning.

Walking out of that bank I felt like an adult! I had my big girl panties on and was taking control of my finances as a single mother. I secured a new car loan and was able to make the payments. At that moment, I was sure that the only thing missing in my life was a relationship. Despite my progress in other areas of my life, I was, unfortunately, still waiting for some white knight to come along and *save* me.

I ultimtely met a man at work, and although the relationship seemed to be going great, he wasn't the least bit open to taking on financial responsibility for me or my kids. At this point in my life, they came first. Hanging on to hope that he would change, I lived with this man in common law for two years, only to find myself dealing with divorce number two.

Parents, husbands, employment, living on my own—none had taught me the basics of credit and debt and budgeting. What I gained from those favors life had afforded me was a continuing unhealthy relationship with money. I started to accumulate credit card debt and lived paycheck-to-paycheck, trying to figure out how to feed my kids. *Where's that financial stability I had in my first marriage?*

Does life send us what we look for? I was keeping my eyes open, waiting to meet White Knight #2, and I did! I met a guy online and we seemed to have so much in common. Also, he helped to pay for some major car expenses for me, and since he worked in the same dealership where I had purchased my car, was able to get me warranty coverage, which saved me thousands of dollars. We dated and moved in together, and I quickly found the financial stability I was looking for. Oh, but wait! There was a problem.

Once again. I don't really love him. I thought it was love, but it's just the security. Will the love come? Will things get worse?

Get worse they did. He lost his job and started his own computer company while I was still working at the grocery store making good money. Once again, credit card debt racked up. He said he was making very little money and deposited what he could in the joint accounts. We even moved to a different city to try another job, but it didn't work out, and he ended up getting a job offer at his original car dealer, as a Manager.

The trouble was the job was on Vancouver Island, where I had no friends. I started feeling a kind of *déjà vu* from my first marriage. If you've had more than one relationship, maybe you can relate to what I was feeling. *I am going to make it work this time, even though everything is screaming inside of me not to do it!*

The "security" of a committed relationship and the shame of not knowing how to make it on my own stopped me in my tracks and left me settling for what I had.

This relationship did not have the physical abuse, but the emotional vacuum he lived in did not work for me either. He expended the emotion he did have dealing with the demons of his own divorce, his ex-wife and her gaining custody of his kids.

Financially, we still struggled. In moving to the Island for his benefit, I had a hard time finding a job. I had two or three jobs that simply didn't work out, until 1997, when I went on a job interview for a sales position with MetLife.

I didn't even really know what Metlife was. Oh, I knew I had some sales experience, and I remember the manager saying I would be selling life insurance. Now that was a subject that I knew all too well! Just a year before, in 1996, my first husband and father of my kids, had died of cancer. He had no life insurance, no will, and no savings set aside. In fact, his new wife had to sell everything to pay off their debt.

I guess pain has to be significant before we are open to learning the lesson intended, in this case, Lesson #5: **The importance of having life insurance and a will.** When my ex-husband died, my boys were twelve and fourteen, and for those of you who have kids, you know they are not cheap. The child support I received from him was no longer coming and the government survivor benefit that replaced it was maybe a third of what he had been paying. At the time, I was working in a shared office with a financial planner who got me into an affordable life insurance plan and a lawyer who helped me get a will in place.

Whether it was life's favors, divine intervention, or dumb luck, I started selling life insurance and did very well, drawing on my recent experience of the consequences of not having it.

This is where my story gets a bit surreal. While doing laundry one day, I look in my husband's pocket and find a bank chit with a checking account balance of $42,000. What? You know in the movies when the unsuspecting wife finds lipstick on a collar or a girl's phone number in a pocket? Just like that! Here I was, scraping by to feed the kids on my commission wages and what little he was depositing into our joint account, and there he was, with a whole other account—where did all of that money come from?

When I asked him, he said that he was saving for a house and he was doing it for us!

Thoughts raced through my mind. *A house, which we had not talked about, my kids eating ramen noodles and Kraft dinner because that is what I can afford, and he drops this on me?*

I found out that he was writing personal cheques from his own account into our joint account. He had said they were his pay checks, when in reality he made up the amounts as he saw fit.

Wow! Here I was facing yet another tidal wave, a tsunami that knocked me off my feet and left looking right up at Lesson #6: **Have a money talk with your spouse.** It is essential that each member of a couple knows how much the other makes, how much debt is accrued, and what is in place both for spending and saving plans.

At that time, it was too late for a money talk, so our marriage ended soon after my laundry discovery. Despite everything, I was grateful that we did not buy a house together. Small miracles!

Six months after that divorce, I still struggled, not sure how to balance commission income with taking care of my household finances. A key component of getting paid that way is budgeting for when you don't have the current sales to pay your bills. Oops—I didn't get that lesson!

As I attempted to manage money between commissions, once again the debt started to look like a huge mountain range surrounding me. I was doing well enough in sales, but there was not a predictable pay every two weeks. A blessing came when my manager recognized my leadership skills and asked me to step up as a trainer and be part of the management team. I thought I had gone to heaven! I loved my job, and now it took care of my security, in the form of a regular paycheck. But self doubt still plagued me.

How is it I can have a great job and not really be happy with my life? I have accumulated so much debt and after three failed relationships, I am starting to believe the problem is me!

Well it was, but at that point in time, I only knew what I knew.

In the midst of turmoil, I received another major blessing, in the form of one of the advisors I worked with. We were the same age and both divorced single moms, but the similarities ended there. A successful advisor, she made six figures, owned her own home after a divorce, drove a Chrysler New Yorker, dressed well and was quite confident being in her own skin. I remember saying to her, "It must be nice to have all of this! How did you do it?"

"You can have it too Shari," she said, "and I'll show you how."

As this generous mentor took me under her wing, I suddenly realized I had lost myself. I was a mother, daughter, sister, wife, friend, but who was Shari?

I think Shari was lost on that weekend when I was eighteen. Maybe earlier. I don't know. I don't remember things clearly, and my parents tell me two distincly different stories about my past. Regardless, here I was twenty-one years later, saying, "Hello Shari, nice to meet you! Now, let's get to work."

Being mentored included an introduction to a life motivated by the wisdom of Tony Robbins and Brian Tracy, to name a few. I engaged in their programs and was elated to see my life changing, seemingly overnight. Most importantly, I was taught how to set goals.

Here I am, 39 years old, and I've never written a goal down!

I still have the list of those first goals that I documented. Some came to fruition and some did not, but the power was in the documenting. Riding this wave was fun, and I learned four words that changed my life: **Ink what you think**!

With all the support and mentoring, I reaped other rewards. I lost fifty pounds, was able to get my debt paid down, and best of all, I was a better mother for my kids, a better friend, and better mentor and trainer in my profession.

I paid it forward to my advisors and taught them about goal setting. So that we all could give each other's goals energy, I even started a dream board for us. As a particular example, let me tell you about my dream car. I envisioned a bright, shiny Mercedes Kompress convertible.

One of my friends took me to the Mercedes dealership and had me test drive the car and I'll never forget that day. Not only had I vividly imagined it, but there I was, driving it. It just wasn't mine... yet. I took the brochure I brought home that day and cut out the car. I then cut out my picture and put myself in the driver's seat (ha-ha, literally), and it went on my dream board.

Side note: Within two years, I was ready to own that Mercedes. Since my golf clubs wouldn't fit, I got a silver Mustang convertible instead, which I also loved and which fit my life. Sometimes the results of goal setting are different and even better than you imagined. Now back to that story.

I was still single and actually okay with that. I sat myself down and decided I could put romance on the back burner. I knew it was finally time to work on me, and a man in my life would only serve to distract me.

Life frequently lifts us with surprises; shortly after the heart-to-heart conversation with myself, I met my current husband. Our journey has not been all peaches and roses; marriage is hard work and we still have our differences.

But I've realized that if I'm open to learning, I can find lessons everywhere, inside a marriage and inside my own heart.

A Few Lessons To Grow On

TO MAINTAIN A healthy marriage let me reiterate: never hesitate to have the money talk. What is the budget? Who pays for what? Which will be joint accounts? What will you invest? How does your partner feel about money? What attitudes and personality traits come to the union? I found I am a "think on my feet and get it done" type of gal. I definitely like spending money, and I'm a risk taker.

My new spouse, on the other hand, grew up with a single mom who was very bitter about me being in her son's life. As I was to learn later, her life was one that had calloused both her and her son toward any entrepreneurial person who would take risks. In her experience, entrepreneurs lie, steal your money, and don't help you with supporting your family. These things represented his dad who, in his eyes, equaled a snake.

When the company I worked for got bought by another big company, many things in our lives changed, and we had to confront our money personalities and issues. The new management was all about profits, period. My manager was dismissed, and the company brought in a young, eager manager who was all about status. He thought my dream board was a joke. His words? "Just get the whip out and get them selling!"

My thoughts? *Uh oh, oil and water are not going to mix!*

I soon found myself being pushed out to make room for more of his buddies who were just like him. I remained with the company just under a year, and I knew I could no longer stay. The company's morals, ethics and management style had slowly changed and I was no longer a good fit. So I left behind a six figure income and went into business for myself. The choice felt right, but still I wondered, *what was I thinking?*

My husband sure had those thoughts.

Life favored me once again, in the form of a friend who had his own broker business. He took me under his wing and helped me take my own business to six figures in two years. How?

Because of my experiences, I came to realize there was a serious missing piece in financial planning. No one taught or talked about the emotional part of it! But I had been teaching up to twenty-five advisors how to tap into their dreams and hearts to get to what really mattered to them, and it worked. That's where the real planning starts. Unfortunately, traditional financial planning today is still based only on what our grandparents were taught: Spend less than you make, and save at least ten percent of your income to invest in your future retirement.

I believe that particular mindset worked for them because they didn't have the convenience of plastic. There were no debit cards, credit cards, layaway plans, or don't-pay-for-one-year plans, and most people worked toward healthy pensions. They usually worked for one, maybe two companies, and that was it. If you didn't have the money to buy something, you simply did without it.

The world changed; unfortunately the financial services industry did not. It still preaches the same old basic foundations to all consumers. The "spend less, earn more, and invest and save" philosophy remains perfectly good advice. Why it no longer works is that most people have no idea how to achieve those three seemingly simple tasks! Most people don't drive benefit from healthy financial education from our parents or peers, and are relegated to continue to find their way by braille, just like I did.

Through the mentoring of my friend with the broker business, I learned to manage money based on my hopes and dreams, those which fit the the self I had lost and finally found again. I also took into account myriad limiting money beliefs I didn't even know I had. I found a new passion to start groups for women to help educate them to take ownership of their own finances.

I knew first hand that in many families, men take care of the money, while women are embarrassed and feeling inadaquate in their own skills.

As I worked with more women, my main words of reassurance became, "When you know better, you do better. Where you currently are is not your fault, but now get over yourself and get help; it's a sign of strength to take control of your life."

Once you have been taught basic financial management, once you know the "how," it's both easy and freeing!

Riding Smoother Waves

I'M GOING INTO my tenth year as an entrepreneur, and my success has left a trail. The journey to take control of my finances and life was a long one, and included some essential steps I had to take to get here. The following are the steps, tips, and actions that I believe every self-employed business owner needs to take as well.

If you are married, to best benefit the lives of everyone involved, **have the support of your significant other**. Otherwise, the lack of support will eventually bite you in the backside when times get tough and the money drains more rapidly than it fills your coffers. Having your own business is taking a risk and both you and your partner have to be comfortable with that.

Have a buffer account for your business for when finances become stressed. Too many people fail to plan and and find themselves just "winging it" in their businesses, not realizing one little hiccup can take them down.

Do you **know your numbers**? Not only in your business, but more importantly the more personal numbers within your home. There will be nothing short of problems if you are not aware of your day-to-day expenses, along with those of your business. You must always know not only where your money is going, but from where and how much is coming in.

Do you **have a plan and regularly set financial goals** in your business and your life? Like myself, too many people out there don't have a financial education and are now trying to run a business. It will eventually catch up with you, like it did with me after my third divorce. Nothing more than the lack of a plan took me right to the bottom where for a while, I couldn't see any light, took me to the place where I finally saw I needed help and was not able to do it by myself. Speaking of which...

You will need to **hire the services** of any important team member necessary to grow your business, whether that is a coach or consultant, web designer or assistant. I tried to do it all by myself for the first two years, and even though financially I did fine, I now realize I would have done even better if I had let go of some of the administrative tasks, thinking I was saving money, but that ultimately kept me from doing what I do best, selling and generating revenue.

Today I know that I would not have found financial success in business if I hadn't been splashed or knocked down by all of those waves of many years of lessons. My hope is that your journey can be a bit steadier.

What I've learned makes me passionate to help others, and with the benefit of my own experience, to help them find financial success more quickly. The real key to abundance in life and in business is **tapping into your heart and what is truly important to you**. Why are you in business? Why do you do what you do? What legacy do you want to leave? What do you experience when you connect your head to your heart in your business?

When you know your heart, you're suddenly aware that you are meant to be doing what you are doing, and when you operate from that place of purpose, nothing can stop you!

A Final Lesson

HERE'S WHAT I know; I have learned a lot of people are living with pain, and it shows up in their business as lack of sales, lack of focus, struggle, or unhappiness, amongst other things.

This pain itself is not usually on the surface. As it was for me, it's often buried, and because people haven't yet "owned it," they do nothing to change it.

Convincing ourselves we don't feel it creates even more suffering.

This is a lonely place to be—living with hidden shame, guilt and embarrassment, about money and more. If this is where you are, you might be feeling like you're the only one. Well, you're not.

Get together with a professional, and fix this money mess right now. Take your power back by drawing on the support of another to guide you through to a new perspective. From there, you can be the source of inspiration for others.

A final lesson: **If I can do it, so can you!** You can peel away the layers of impossibility and travel down a new path, headed right towards your dreams, whatever they are. Once you know the source of your pain, you can find a solution.

This is also what I believe, and this is what my heart says is true. What I've shared with you here is my core set of values, passions, and beliefs, all of which I discovered by uncovering the source of my pain as well as the source of my power.

I leave you with this: You are never alone, and living a bigger life is so possible for you. Life is short, so I urge you... don't settle and don't wait to tap into the knowing of your heart. Abundance is here and now, for you—whether that is personally or professionally.

About The Author

Shari Molchan wants to live in a world where all women can create financial independence. A down-to-earth Financial Advisor + Money Relationship Specialist, she's been spotlighted on eWomen Network, Women Warriors Radio, International Life Coach Radio and *Unemployable Woman Magazine.* When she's not demystifying money for unstoppable women, you can find her working on lowering her golf handicap, sipping a glass of wine with the girls, or chasing the grand babies. Her first book, *Maximum Money Momentum*, was released on February 2012; there is an encore in the works.

Contract:
www.sharimolchan.com
shari@molchanfinancial.com

Face The Fear of The Unknown

How I Came To Be An Abundant Wellness Coach

Lisa Marie Pepe

You gain strength, courage, and confidence by every experience in which you really stop to look fear in the face. You are able to say to yourself, 'I lived through this horror. I can take the next thing that comes along.

~ Eleanor Roosevelt (1884 – 1962)
American politician, diplomat, and activist.

C ongratulations, my friend! You have been inspired to pick up this book, and have no doubt, continued reading until now because there is something inside of you that has been stirring for awhile... perhaps you've been toying with the idea of making a career transition or perhaps the seed has been planted that you are being called to give life a bigger and better you. Or perhaps you've been looking for a "sign" that you are on the right path to wherever it is you're supposed to be. Well, look no further.

This is your sign, right here, right now! Whether you're still on the fence or ready to get up and go, the best is yet to come!

I am honored to share my story with you and it is my most sincere hope that after reading it, you will feel inspired to get up and get started on your own journey towards building the life of your dreams! I want you to gain practical hands-on knowledge that you can apply in your business endeavors, but more importantly, I want you to believe at the very core of your being that you have what it takes to turn your dreams into reality... that you can be abundantly you, on purpose in business.

Make the commitment now! Dig your heels in deep and get ready for the ride of a lifetime! Keep reading, my friend; you're well on your way!

There Are No Guarantees In Life

HOW MANY TIMES have you heard the old cliché, "There are no guarantees in life?" If you're like most people, you've probably heard it more times than you care to remember. That's probably because someone who was trying to console you, following a personal loss or setback of some sort, uttered it to you. While the same cliché is often overheard in big corporate meeting rooms and small business break rooms, nothing could be further from the truth.

In life as in business, you are guaranteed to face challenges along the way.
~ Lisa Marie Pepe

You are guaranteed to have setbacks; you are guaranteed to have questions... guaranteed to feel overwhelmed. And are guaranteed to have days when you absolutely feel like giving up altogether. It's understandable; trust me. I've been there, too. The one thing, however, which you must never do in this lifetime, is give up on yourself or your dreams, ever!

Moving From Plan A To Plan B

IF PLAN A doesn't work out, learn from it and move on to Plan B. If Plan B doesn't work out, well... remember you've got an entire alphabet to work with. Above all else, reach out to your Divine Creator, whatever you conceive Him to be, during your times of struggle. I'm very spiritual and I know that God has always given me just enough light for the step I'm on. While I may not been able to see the light at the end of the tunnel... at least there has been enough illumination to take the next step. Whether in personal or business affairs, my belief in God has enabled me to keep going. My advice to you:

No matter where you are right at this moment, continue reading the words that flowed effortlessly and directly from my heart to you.

~ Lisa Marie Pepe

When the opportunity to step up and participate, as a contributing author for this anthology was first presented to me, I was both humbled and honored. At first, the fearless prayer warrior inside of me said, "Wow! This is an amazing opportunity. You've been praying... you asked for abundance and the Universe has replied, "Jump right in and start writing. You've got what it takes." Just as I was about to sign the contract though, the little voice of self-doubt crept in with its same old self-defeating messages, causing me to hesitate.

As with any other major life decision, I decided to take a step back and to clear my mind. I meditated upon my decision. I prayed. I asked other writers for their advice and I looked for the "signs from above" that had always seemed to appear when I needed them most. Of course, the "signs" didn't come right away, but sure enough they came... not a moment too late and not a moment too soon, but just in time. When I felt I had enough clarity, I picked up the phone immediately and called my editor. Without any hesitancy I declared, "Sign me up. I'm ready to go."

Looking back now, I realize that this choice, by far, was one of the wisest choices I've made both for my personal and professional development. Not only have I been given a platform to share my expertise with the world, but I've also been blessed with meeting so many other fascinating, positive-minded, and passionate folks with whom I have much in common with. It is with great honor that I share my journey of becoming a Certified Wellness Coach with you, in hopes that you are inspired to take the next step and begin living the life of your dreams.

When Life Changes Your Direction

IT WAS MAY 25, 2011 and I was driving home from the day spa where I worked as a Licensed Massage

Therapist. Although I was relatively new to the field, I absolutely loved what I did and felt like I was at "home" for the first time in a very long time in my professional career... little did I know that on that evening my life was suddenly about to change. As I was driving home on the interstate and about to exit, I was suddenly side-swiped on the driver's side by a speeding truck, which never even stopped to see if I was okay. With pure adrenaline coursing through my veins, I managed to follow the driver and finally got him to pull over. Although I was shaken up, I wasn't terribly injured in the sense that you might think so I refused medical attention and promised the State Police Officer that I would get checked out in the morning.

When I woke up the next day I was sore as expected and preceded to speak with an attorney who advised me to get X-Rays and an evaluation for physical therapy, which I did immediately. Although the X-Ray did not reveal any structural damage to my neck or shoulder, I was diagnosed with a cervical sprain and began physical therapy that same day. I was also advised to remain out of work and to refrain from going to the gym until I was medically cleared. At the time, I was in the best physical shape of my life and figured it would only be about a week before things got back to normal... but was I wrong!

Nothing from that day forward returned to *normal* as I had known it to be. I followed all the of the doctor's orders and yet I still didn't feel "right." I'll never forget the excruciating discomfort and spasms I felt shoot up my left arm and through my neck, when I attempted to go back to work about two weeks later. I struggled through the massage session and broke down and cried when I got into the break room. My boss consoled and told me to go home and rest and to return when I was fully healed. I was grateful for her kindness and words of encouragement, but I was frustrated as hell. I was "supposed" to be better by now. I was "supposed" to be healed and fully ready to go back to the life I had come to love and know. Little did I know, but the day I left the spa marked the first day of what would be a long and winding road...

When I arrived home that night, I took a hot shower to relieve the spasms along with a few ibuprofen, and applied some topical analgesic to my neck and left shoulder. I felt better for the moment, but I was still concerned that something just didn't feel right. I met with my physical therapist the next day and he referred me to an orthopedic surgeon for further evaluation. I had an MRI of my cervical spine and my left shoulder only to be told by the orthopedic surgeon that, "Well, nothing showed up on the tests so you're going to have to take it easy until the muscles heal. It can take a long time sometimes, but you'll be OK. In the meantime, no heavy lifting or intense exercise, and definitely no working out." As I left the orthopedics' office, part of me felt somewhat relieved that at least nothing was wrong structurally, so to speak, but the other part of me began to panic. What was I going to do next?

When Fear Immobilizes You

AS THE ANXIETY started to creep in, I found myself starting to imagine the worst of the worst. I wasn't used to being knocked down, at least not for long. Up until this point, I had never had an injury that kept me out of commission for more than a few days at best. In the blink of an eye though, the days turned into weeks and the weeks into months; I still couldn't get my groove back. I tried a combination of Western and Eastern medical remedies including high doses of prescription anti-inflammatory medications, cortisone injections, ice, heat, massage therapy, chiropractic care, and even acupuncture, but nothing seemed to provide lasting relief. Several weeks after "finishing" my physical therapy, I decided to give it my best shot. Although I really wasn't physically capable, I made one last attempt to prove to myself that I could power through the discomfort to perform my duties as a massage therapist.

After trying to return to the physical demands of the job one last time, I decided it was time to let go and acknowledge that I was probably never going back to the profession I had grown to love. That day, I officially resigned; not sure of what or where I was headed next, I wept as I drove home. Actually, I did more than weep. I broke down physically and emotionally; I cried... I panicked... I felt lost and I didn't know what to do. The two things I enjoyed most, my profession and my endorphin rush from working out, were suddenly gone.

I continued with all the recommended treatments, but to no avail. My mind, my body, and more importantly, my spirit, felt broken. I knew that I would eventually find my way again, but for the time being all I could do was wait... wait until my body and my mind were ready to start over... again.

As it turned out, I had actually torn the cartilage in my left shoulder, but it was never detected in the first MRI... only two years later, after years of going from doctor to doctor, trying everything under the sun to get better, was I diagnosed with a tear in the labrum of my shoulder. To earn a living in the meantime, I took mundane, meaningless task-oriented jobs, and feeling more miserable about myself nearly every day. Here I was... two graduate degrees, neither of which I wanted to pursue and one passion which I was no longer capable of doing... a good friend approached me at work one day and asked, "Lisa, what are you doing?"

Oblivious to her question, I replied, "Emptying the trash like I'm supposed to."

"No. What are you really doing? I mean here— working here for minimum wage when you have so much more to offer the world."

I looked to my friend and replied, "I don't know. It's been so long since I've done any teaching or clinical work that I wouldn't even know where to begin."

"Well, you best figure it out, Miss Lisa before your life passes you by. Go home and think about what I said."

The Shift From Confusion To Clarity

I LEFT WORK that summer evening feeling even more confused about life than usual, but I knew at that moment that my friend had reignited in me the flame, which had been extinguished years before. Within two months of that conversation, I successfully pursued getting a full-time teaching position for the upcoming academic year. By the grace of God and with the help and encouragement of family and friends, I was offered a full-time position—as a special education para professional. I gladly accepted the offer and was elated to begin working full-time again in the field of education... except that darn shoulder injury wasn't getting any better. Fast-forward three years: after multiple X-Rays and two MRI's, it was confirmed that my only option to repair the torn cartilage in my shoulder was to undergo arthroscopic surgery.

On January 21, 2014 I went in for arthroscopic surgery to repair a torn labrum in my left shoulder. I knew ahead of time that this procedure could take anywhere from six months to a year or more to fully rehabilitate, but I was *determined* to beat the odds. I had already informed my employer that I'd be back to work in two weeks. I figured... how bad could it be? A little shoulder surgery couldn't keep me down, right?

Wrong! I was informed when I awoke there was much more damage in the joint than what had been previously seen on an MRI and that a comprehensive open shoulder reconstruction had taken place instead. Against my surgeon's recommendations as well as those made by my family and friends, I made the effort with my arm in a sling and pinned to my chest to return to work on "light duty" only two weeks after surgery.

Looking back now I realize how foolish it was for me to even attempt to return to work, but as they say, "hindsight is 50/50." Within hours of being up and out the door, my body let me know that it was definitely too soon to be back. I managed to struggle through the day, holding back the tears I desperately needed to shed. By the time I got to the car, the tears were flowing freely down my face; my body was in extreme discomfort and my mind was riddled with anxiety. Unsure of how long it would take for me to get back to the profession of working with special education students, into which I had recently transitioned, I let the tears flow. After composing myself and reaching out to my family and friends for their advice, I made arrangements that day to remain out on a medical leave of absence for the next month.

Luckily, my surgeon and my family and friends were highly supportive of my decision, rather than condemning me for trying to return in the first place.

The next four weeks, while I remained out of work, were the most mentally, physically, and emotionally challenging days in my life to date. Due to the type of surgery I had, my shoulder had to remain pinned for six full weeks before I could even start physical therapy. During this time, I was unable to fully take care of myself. I couldn't sleep in my bed, drive, bathe, cook, or even dress myself! Me... the person so used to being very independent, suddenly for the first time in my adult life, being was at the mercy of those around me. Even the simplest life necessity of taking a shower was an overwhelming task, which required assistance on all levels.

I am extremely grateful that I had my parents, my boyfriend, and my friends to help me with the simplest tasks of daily living. I also couldn't workout at the gym or practice yoga like I had been doing prior to the surgery. To make matters worse, we had one of the most brutal New England winters we'd had in a long time. It seemed like every other day we were hit with a Nor'easter—as we like to refer to them here. For those of you who are not from New England, a Nor'easter is the same as a blizzard, but with a lot of extra wind to accompany it. Talk about being home-bound and feeling "trapped!"

Finding Your Purpose

EVEN THOUGH I was physically uncomfortable, I got bored very easily. In order to conquer the boredom, I found small "projects" to keep myself busy... like reading, playing games on my tablet, and chatting on the phone with friends, old and new. I had never been a couch potato, so sitting around and watching daytime TV was not an option. I started listening to music and compiling a list of positive quotes and uplifting messages.

Little did I know at the time these collectives would later be used in launching my own wellness coaching business. Many of my little "projects" helped, but for someone as active as myself, they simply weren't enough to keep me from going stir-crazy. I'd be remiss to not tell you that from time to time I fought off the fears of insecurity that kept creeping into my mind while I was laid up and out of commission. With the love and support of my parents, my boyfriend and a few close friends, I managed to make it through the next several weeks without going completely bonkers.

About a month later I started physical therapy. I felt scared and excited at the same time as I arrived at the physical therapy office. On one hand, I so desperately wanted to get better and back to being my old self, but on the other, I had heard horror stories from nearly every person I knew who had shoulder surgery that the rehabilitation part could be downright torturous!

I'll never forget how I felt the first time the therapist went to bend my elbow after having had it pinned for six weeks. I winced in agony as he gently moved my arm away from my side! On a scale of 1-10 I'd say my discomfort level hit the 100 mark without question!

Although we hadn't accomplished much more than an assessment during my first visit, I left the office that day, thinking, *how on Earth am I going to make it through this process? At least another recommended six months of this bloody hell? How am I going to do this and go back to work at the same time?* Once again, the insecurities crept in... *What if I can't go back to work? What if I am forced to remain home for the next several months? How will I pay my bills? What if I don't heal? What if I do heal?* What if... what if... what if? Every insecurity and fear ran through my mind, and then... it hit me! From deep within, a gentle voice whispered to me:

Lisa, take care of yourself... you need time to rest, to heal, to repair.
You need this time for yourself. Everything will work out. It will be okay.

I applied for a non-paid medical leave of absence through the remainder of the academic year, which thankfully, I was granted. I also made arrangements to curb my spending and to ask for financial help from my family. Although the basics had been covered, I still needed a purpose... that is something to live for other than to "just wake-up" every day, do physical therapy, and be alone with my own thoughts and insecurities.

Look For The Possibilities

CURIOUS BY NATURE and always interested in health and wellness, I started to utilize my time more productively. I searched the web to educate myself more about topics related to health and wellness, I read numerous articles about the mind-body connection and spoke to myriad other like-minded professionals. One afternoon, as I was reading an article on foods that promote healing after surgery, which just so happened to be written by a wellness coach, a light bulb went off! That same afternoon, I began research on how I could use my current skills to help others find their "purpose" in life.

After many hours of surfing the web and talking with folks from all over the country, I chose to complete the Wellness Coaching Certification Program with the Spencer Institute for Life Coaching. I had the time and the motivation; why not? Over the next several weeks I made it my mission to eat, sleep, and breathe the in's and out's of wellness coaching. I was determined to take advantage of the time I had to pursue my new goal and this time... I did! After many hours of intense, dedicated study I passed the final exam for the course and became a Certified Wellness Coach! I'll never forget the feeling I had when I opened the envelope from the Spencer Institute and first saw the title "Certified Wellness Coach" after my name. For the first time in a long time I felt like I had found my life's purpose again. Little did I know that at that moment I was about to embark on yet another journey, only this time the focus would be on reinventing myself and building a brand new career.

I'll be the first person to admit that when I first ventured out into the world of professional wellness coaching I had absolutely no clue as to what I was doing or how I was going to do it! In fact, the only thing I knew was that I had an authentic passion and deep burning desire to empower other people to feel good about themselves. During the initial business-building phase, there were days, weeks, and even months when I felt overwhelmed and frustrated. Hell, there were days when I even felt like giving up altogether and throwing in the towel, but I didn't. You may be asking yourself, "Well that's great to know you **did** it, but how did you **do** it?" Well, the answer is quite simple, but the process is somewhat complex. Simply stated, I held onto my faith in God, which allowed me to have faith in myself.

Don't Waste Time—Get Going

ONCE I RECEIVED my official certification, I didn't waste much time! I was ready to get started as soon as possible, except… I didn't have much experience in business! I knew I wanted an official business name… a website… and a handful of matching business cards. I had an idea of what I wanted to name my business, but I bounced a couple of possibilities off my family and closest friends before finding the "right" one.

Ultimately, I chose the name "Positive Transformation Personal Wellness Coaching" for my business because it just seemed to flow very naturally and felt like a "good fit" to match my purpose and my passion.

I asked a few friends who were website developers what the first step was in creating a website and was informed that I needed a secured domain before I could do anything else. I checked online to see if "Positive Transformation" was an available domain for a website; thankfully, it was.

I jumped on the chance to secure the domain name through Go Daddy even though I had not a single clue how to build a website. Given that I was operating on a very limited budget and could not afford to pay a website designer to create my website, I utilized as many free resources as possible, including the Go Daddy Technical Support Team.

A firm believer in the Law of Attraction, I snagged a piece of notebook paper and literally wrote out: "I am launching my website two weeks from now." Although I hadn't a clue as to how I would do it, I knew that once I made the declaration to get it done, I would find a way to complete the task. I told others about my goal and even posted my declaration on my social media profiles. I knew that doing so would help me stay on track and keep me accountable as people would inevitably ask, "How's that website coming along?"

The next two weeks, I literally ate, slept, and breathed the build out of my website. Of course, being a wellness coach, I also made time to take care of myself by eating well, exercising each day, and getting enough quality sleep, but still I worked whole-heartedly! I even became quite friendly with the Go Daddy Support Team during that entire time, usually chatting with a representative once or twice per day and sometimes more if I needed to. Although I wanted my website to be a unique representation of the depth of my purpose and passion, I also consulted with other life coaches and asked them for feedback along the way. I even showed several versions of it to family and friends before I decided to publish it. While I made slight adjustments here and there based on the feedback I received, I trusted my instinct for much of the project.

Finally, after about two and a half weeks of working feverishly, I felt somewhat satisfied with the website I had created, keeping in mind that I could always go back and modify or edit various sections as I evolved in my career. Once I was ready to make the website go live however, I hovered over that "Launch Website Now" button for quite some time! Perhaps it was the fear of failure that held me back... or maybe it was the fear of success. Either way, I was hesitant for a few moments, but I knew I needed to move forward. Eventually, I convinced myself that I had done the best I could and clicked on the option to make my website visible to the online world. I even scheduled a "Website Launch Party" event on Facebook to help me really get the word out more efficiently. I asked for honest feedback and much to my surprise, I received a lot of positive comments, along with some helpful and constructive tips on how to make my website that much better.

Looking back now, I realize now the process of building my website from scratch was a daunting task, no doubt, but it was also an invaluable learning experience. Not only had I set out to accomplish the task at hand, but had taught myself how to do something completely new. Turns out, it was amongst one of the best decisions I made in the very early stages of my career as it not only helped me become visible within the eyes of the public, but it also helped me to feel more confident in myself and my ability to make my dreams of becoming a wellness coach that much more tangible. Most importantly, it was the starting point of a whole new adventure in Business Building 101.

Developing Key Strategies

AS THE WEEKS progressed, I knew that staying organized and focused were paramount if I were truly serious about making a living as a wellness coach. In an effort to carve out a niche for myself, I developed a few key strategies, which I've aptly named, *The Core Five to Building a Successful Business;* doing a deep dive into Curiosity, Courage, Commitment, Collaboration, and Confidence. It is with great humility and privilege I share my blueprint for success with you.

Curiosity

YES! BE CURIOUS. Be hungry for knowledge. Be a life-long learner. Be a risk-taker, within reason, and above all else, ask questions. If you feel uncomfortable asking others directly for answers to your questions, jot them down on a notepad and conduct your own research. You don't have to share them with anyone other than yourself. Remember, there is no such thing as a stupid question. No matter which field you are in or how experienced you are, there will always be new things to learn.

With the efficiency of social media these days, it is fairly easy to find the answers to many of your most pressing questions. Google and YouTube are excellent free resources where you can find the answers to just about anything your imagination can conceive. Be fearless. Be bold. Be daring.

Above all else, dig your heels in deep and research every topic imaginable related to your field. You can educate yourself by surfing the web for credible resources, reading articles that are relevant to your area of interest and/or signing up for informative webinars, many of which cost nothing more to join than your time. Applying these principles, especially in the very early stages of building my business, proved to be one of the most effective uses of my time. Surprisingly, many of the topics I later researched and ultimately employed in the development of my business were actually available for free right from the start! Although it took many hours of sifting through various online articles, webinars, and podcasts to find those that were best for me, I couldn't think of a better way to have invested my time.

Courage

MANY PEOPLE ARE afraid to ask others for what they truly need for fear that they'll be rejected, laughed at, or ignored altogether. Sound familiar? Know anyone like this? Perhaps it's you. If so, you are not alone. Many people have a difficult time asking for advice or help when they need it most. This is especially true of new business owners who are just starting out. What you may not realize, however, is that when you fail to ask, the answer will always be, without any doubt, "No."

However, if you are willing to step outside your comfort zone, even if just for a moment, and ask for a little help along the way, there is at least a slight possibility that you might get the answers you were seeking all along.

Therefore, never hesitate to ask for guidance from those that have already traveled the path you are about to venture on. After all, even the most experienced and successful business owner started out as a novice... a beginner. Throughout much of my journey, I found many successful wellness coaches who were willing to barter for services and even those who agreed to mentor me completely pro bono. All they asked was that "I pay it forward" in due time, which I humbly agreed to do.

Commitment

LET'S BE REALISTIC; commitment involves more than just hard work. It requires discipline, action and a consistent effort on your part to work... even when you feel less than enthusiastic to do so. Making a commitment to yourself to do the very best that you can is a great start, but it may not be enough.

Commitment also involves creating ways necessary to hold yourself accountable. One of the best ways I have found to stay committed and focused on a goal is to tell others what it is you want to accomplish, and the time frame in which you would like to accomplish it. I call this the accountability factor. It simply means you share your goals, your dreams, your hopes, your wishes, and anything and everything you want to achieve in your personal life and in your business... with your family and your closest friends.

As you continue to work towards achieving your goals, ask your family and friends for their help along the way; ask them to call you once or twice a week or to shoot you a text message or email every two days or so. Whenever I made an arrangement such as this, I found I was significantly more productive; I always knew my supporters were going to be checking in with me and the last thing I wanted to do was inform them I hadn't made any progress in the time since we last spoke! Hence, the accountability factor, when enforced, can help keep you accountable and help you to stay focused and on track, especially on the dark, gloomy days when all you really want to do is give up.

Collaboration

IT HAS BEEN my fortunate experience as a fairly new entrepreneur and Certified Wellness Coach that the art of collaboration is one of the best ways to work effectively and efficiently to get the job done. Since starting out in this field, I have witnessed firsthand, the amazing results of collaborating with others. In truth, I attribute the art of collaboration as one of the major factors that has enabled me to reach the level of success I've reached thus far.

Shortly after launching my website, I was contacted by someone from the Life Coach Radio Network (LCRN) who asked me if I was interested in joining the larger group. I had never heard of the LCRN, but I decided to do a bit of research to see if it was a worthwhile cause. What I discovered amazed me!

A week later, I contacted the same person who had initially reached out to me and officially joined the LCRN. Looking back, I realize that joining the LCRN early on in my career was by far the best decision I made. Since doing so, not only have I gained some healthy media exposure, but I've also had the opportunity to meet and collaborate with several life coaches from all different walks of life.

As a matter of fact, some of my closest friends and colleagues are those that I first met when I joined the LCRN. Not long after co-hosting just a few weekly shows, I started to feel more confident about myself, and my ability to be an effective coach.

One of the other things that I found to be really helpful in the initial stages of my career was to make a conscious decision be open to whatever opportunities would present themselves. As an advocate of the Law of Attraction, I firmly believe whatever thoughts I put out into the universe will eventually come to fruition. Not surprisingly, as soon as I made the decision to become a Certified Wellness Coach I surrounded myself with inspirational quotes and images that would ultimately attract me to the very people who needed my service. Sure enough, I started to "find" others who wanted to either hire me as their coach or collaborate with me on larger projects.

It seems as though one opportunity after the next began to pop up out of the blue. Other life coaches, inspirational speakers, and writers in the health and wellness field started to contact me. When asked how they had first seen my name, I was told that it was because they had either seen my profile on Facebook, Twitter, or LinkedIn or had heard me speak on the radio. One opportunity turned into another. As I began to feel more confident in my own skin, I started to network more frequently. I even joined additional professional networking groups on Facebook, Twitter and LinkedIn that were comprised mostly of life coaches, inspirational speakers and writers. The more groups I courageously joined and interacted with, the more connections I made. The more connections I made, the more authentic I began to feel.

If someone asks you to take the risk toget involved in a collaborative project, the little voices of insecurity will surely pop right in to tell you all of the reasons why you're not qualified for the task at hand. Ignore them! Stand up tall and face yourself in the mirror and have a little "talk with self!"

You have what it takes to get the job done! You must believe that you are being called on by others to collaborate because they've seen something in you that makes you stand out as an expert in your field.

~ Lisa Marie Pepe

This is yet another example of how the Law of Attraction operates. If you don't already know what it is that you'll need in order to get the job done, have no worries, the Universe will respond!

Remember, we live in an automated world where you can master almost anything by utilizing multiple free resources such as Google and YouTube, amongst many others. If someone approaches you to be a guest speaker on their radio show or webinar, take it. You may not be the most eloquent public speaker, but it's an opportunity to hone in on speaking and presentation skills, not to mention bolstering visibility, credibility and confidence. If there are professional and trusted organizations within your field that you'd like to join, but can't afford, ask if there's any way to barter for services. I am a big proponent of bartering because there's always something you are going to be able to do better than someone else and vice versa. It's always best if you can trade services as opposed to exchanging service for a fee.

Don't sell yourself short! When you create your social media profiles, be sure to highlight your areas of expertise. Sure you're not going to be an expert on everything, but that's OK. Always place your title after your name. Yes, it may feel really awkward when someone first refers to you as an expert; my thoughts... *Hell, it evens feels a little awkward for me sometimes to say that I'm a Certified Wellness Coach.* You'll be pleasantly surprised, though, as you consistently work to market yourself. Sooner than later you will attract the right people into your life to help you on your journey. I know this to be true because time and time again I have experienced it on a personal and professional level.

Once I joined the LCRN, I started to attract people who are just like me; people who share the same passion for health, wellness, and helping others. I began to follow my colleagues from the LCRN on various social media platforms and they, in turn, began to follow me. I can't tell you how much of an invaluable resource it has been to affiliate myself with some of the top experts in my field.

If you haven't yet figured out why the powerful act of collaboration is such an essential component in becoming a successful business owner, here is a brief overview:

Simply stated, there is strength is numbers. When two or people come together with a similar dream to achieve a common purpose, good things happen.

~ Lisa Marie Pepe

My advice to you is to take the opportunities that are given to you. When you are given the chance, collaborate with others who share similar interests as you. If the opportunities do not come directly to you, go forth and create your own. Think of something you'd really like to achieve and ask others if they'd be willing to join you along the way. Use the power of social media to connect and network with others. In addition to utilizing Facebook to network with others in your field, I highly recommend you create opportunities and frequently engage with other professionals on Twitter, and LinkedIn.

When it comes to collaborating with others, just do it. If you don't yet have a Facebook profile, create one! If you haven't built a Facebook page for your business, build one! If you haven't set up your Twitter account yet, set it up today! If you don't know how to do any of these things, allow your curiosity to take carry you!

Do a little research; do a lot of research. Do as much as you can on your own, but reach out to others to help you get the task done. Whatever you do, just get it done!

~ Lisa Marie Pepe

Confidence

IN MY OPINION, confidence is most assuredly by far the most important, yet often overlooked, component to achieving your goals. Without it, you set yourself up for something far less than the best possible outcome in your personal and professional affairs. You can be the most educated, well-spoken, and organized person in the world, but without confidence in yourself and your abilities, you may never attain the level of success you desire.

Many new business owners are under the mis-guided assumption they must have every single detail carefully planned out on paper before sharing their gifts and services with the world. Many other new business owners operate under the notion they have to be an expert at everything in their field before they can begin offering their services.

While having a strategic business plan in place and a solid education behind you adds to your credibility as a business owner, they are not the sole determining factors in predicting whether your business venture will ultimately fail or succeed. What matters most is the determination, courage, passion, and perseverance it will take—day in and day out—to ultimately reach your goal.

All of these components boil down to one thing... *confidence*! You must have a deep and unwavering belief in yourself and your abilities. You've made it this far because you are capable and well equipped to handle the task. All of the hard work, time, energy, and money you've invested in yourself and your business won't do much to propel you forward unless you first believe in yourself!

If you struggle with with or lack self-confidence as many people do, find healthful ways to build up your self-assurance. Listen to inspirational podcasts and audio tracks while you exercise or even while you're driving. Utilize Google and YouTube to find inspiring images, quotes, and videos. Read inspiring stories about others who've achieved success; mentally put your self in their shoes! Write your own positive, self-affirming affirmations, such as, "I am confident in myself and my abilities. I have what it takes," and post them in several locations throughout your house and car so that you will be reminded continuously throughout the course of your day. Make it a daily practice, to speak your positive affirmations aloud. Even though you may not feel comfortable at first, you will begin to feel more confident with time and consistency. After all, your mind is your most powerful tool. When you feed it positive thoughts, positive things happen. Confidence also empowers you to feel more equipped to handle the challenges that come along with pursuing your goals.

So, what does all this mean, and what exactly am I trying to convey you? Simply stated: *you already have whatever it takes to turn your dreams into a reality!* Do not be afraid to step out of your comfort zone. Once you've made your intentions clear and declared loudly to the Universe what and who it is you'd like to attract in your life, be prepared. The Universe will hear everything you've said. Waiting until you are 100% confident in your abilities is not going to get you where you want to be. Having just enough confidence to know that you have what it takes, however, will get you on the right road to going there.

Right from the first solid decision to really build your business, make a pact with yourself that you will never ever give up, no matter how difficult it gets! Along the path to pursue your dreams, you will have days when you feel frustrated, overwhelmed, and confused. You may even have moments when you feel like giving up, altogether, but don't! I understand; there were times when I felt the same way, too. During these times, however, it helps to take a step back, close your eyes, and take a deep breath:

> Get on your knees and pray to your Divine Creator for guidance.
>
> Silence your mind and allow the fire within to reignite.
>
> Do what you have to do to get refocused. Remember why you started in the first place.
>
> Let your inner passion be the driving force that gets you over the hurdles.
>
> Never lose sight of your original goal.
>
> Fuel your passion and let it propel you forward into becoming the business owner you set out to be.
>
> Seek out the support you need to keep you focused on your goal.

It may not be easy, but it sure as hell will be worth it in the end. I am a prime example of this principle and that is why I'm an abundant and purpose-filled business owner today! If I can do it, you can, too. Trust me!

In closing, it is my most sincere hope you have been inspired by reading my story. Perhaps what you've read has ignited a spark within you and moved you to take the first (or next) step in building the life of your dreams. If so, get out there and start building today! The longer you wait, the longer it will take. If what you truly desire is meant to be, you will find a way to make it happen. I believe in you... now it's your turn to believe in you, too! It is this innate belief coupled with taking the actions outlined in my chapter that establish the level of being Abundantly you... on purpose in business.

About The Author

Lisa Marie Pepe is a rapidly rising star in the fields of Life Coaching, Certified Wellness and Social Media.

When Lisa Marie founded the Positive Transformation Personal Wellness Coaching program, it was with a deep passion to empower women to fully embrace how beautiful they truly are by providing them with the tools they need to live healthfully, gain more self-confidence, and meet the world on their terms. In addition to personal wellness coaching, Lisa Marie has extensive experience working one-on-one with female entrepreneurs and individuals in Direct Sales, helping them to master the basics of creating a successful online business.

Lisa Marie acknowledges change of any kind is often unsettling at first glance, but she also views change as our greatest teacher... it reveals how strong we truly are and how much we are capable of achieving. She also believes the key to achieving lifelong health and wellness involves setting small, measurable, and attainable goals along the way.

Lisa Marie Pepe has earned the privilege of being a mentor to others; she has extensive experience, having worked as a mental health clinician, educator, and massage therapist over the past 16 years and now finds her true calling in life is to empower others to empower themselves to live happier, healthier, and more fulfilling lives.

An accomplished inspirational author, speaker, and featured radio host on the *Life Coach Radio Network*, Lisa Marie currently resides in Connecticut with her family.

Contact:
www.positivetransformation.net
https://psocial.co/LisaMariePepe/Info
lisa@positivetransformation.net
lisamariepepe@gmail.com

MODULES

The Game We Call Sales

Dean Philpott

"The starting point of all achievement is desire."

~ Napoleon Hill (1883-1970)
American author, new thought movement.

I believe one of the greatest moments in a person's life is when they realize they are truly in harmony with what it is that they are supposed to be doing. Imagine waking up one day in a moment of pure gratitude and shouting from the depth of your soul, "Thank you God! I'm so happy doing what I love to do!"

As I sat and prepared my final edit for this chapter of *Abundantly You,* I felt that very emotion: I Love what I am doing! It's such a major high for me to be able to share some valuable information about sales from the perspective of a #1 Re/Max agent. Even better, my ideas can be translated into any business to help you secure a place in the top 2% of successful people.

You can also share this material with family and friends because after all, the first principle of success in any area of life is to embrace that we are put on this planet to help and be in service to people. So for

God's sake, take what you learn from this chapter and share it with others!

First, you need to understand that awareness must precede change. There is never going to be any one thing you'll do to take you skyrocketing to the top of your industry. Instead, success will arrive thanks to a compilation of many little things done consistently over a longer period of time. There are no silver bullets with me ladies and gentleman, just persistence.

New Lease on Life

WHEN I RETIRED from my real estate practice in 2011 at the ripe old age of 45, I was not only feeling the need for a drastic change but also an overwhelming desire to help others. I decided to take the Robin Sharma "21-Day Greatness Challenge," and after following his advice to write my legacy, my life changed forever. When we put our legacies into words, we see just how powerful our intentions really are. I knew I had a tremendous responsibility to take action.

I finished writing my sales training program 20 Minutes to Platinum one year later, but it wasn't without major challenges and setbacks; however, what's totally ironic is that as I am writing this very sentence, the program itself was placed in my hands for the first time since it was in the first form of energy.

From just a mere thought during the summer of 2013 to a physical form in 2015, it blew my mind to understand how powerful we really are; Our thoughts become things. My mind grasped this truth and I willingly embraced the substance with the "feelings" in my mind. My biggest awareness: *My thoughts are being given substance with each love-based feeling, such as gratitude, peace and well-being; they are becoming "things" I experience as positive events in my days.*

I called my program *20-Minutes to Platinum* because the different levels of achievement are measured in increments. From my experience and from research, it's a huge gap from the people than earn $100K to the coveted $250K (The Platinum Club). Most sales people and realtors get stuck before they reach the Platinum level, and many express burn out and frustration.

However, the research also shows that if you can reach the Platinum Level, your awareness has been raised high enough that you can convert your earnings into any number you wish. It simply becomes a matter of "decision." And being able to repeat what you already know and kepp doing it better than before.

The "20-minute" part of the name is what I feel we can all afford to put towards our growth each day. If you're part of the elite achievers, you will find 20 minutes per day, three times a day, which in the run of a year is equivalent to going to school for nine 40-hour work weeks. That's a lot of education right there! If you can seize upon your biggest, most desired goal and combine it with sufficient desire and persistence, you will gain the results you deserve.

A year from now you will need a telescope to see where you started.

~ Dean Philpott

It all began for me in Whitehorse, Yukon, where I was known as Dean Philpott aka **The Bald Guy**. All my life, I was told that I would make an excellent realtor, so in 2001 I decided to try it on for size. After a few short years in the business, it was quite evident to the world that this was indeed a great fit. It was quoted that the Bald Guy Real Estate Team "redefined and changed the way Real Estate was bought and sold in the North," and I'm honored and humbled to share with you some wisdom I gained along the way.

Sometimes the life of an ambitious Entrepreneur can feel lonely, and it may seem as though no one really understands what you are going through or struggling with. I am here to tell you that is not the case. As you will discover, most top performing sales people have had doubts, and all have gone through some trying times that made them seriously consider changing careers (and maybe even looking for a J-O-B!).

The only reason they succeeded when others didn't is because they never gave up on their growth and learning. *They never gave up on themselves.* The fact that you are reading this book indicates your understanding that you just need that *one last push* to succeed. You want to understand how you can improve your game. The question is, *Are you willing to put in the time and effort necessary?* Of course I understand some of you may be skeptical because you've probably seen and heard a lot from other seminars and classes, but they just haven't produced the results you want.

I, too, have been to an endless number of "motivational" conferences; I've cheered with other people who have recommitted (repeatedly), and I've tried pretty much everything to improve my numbers, but still... my sales weren't where I wanted them to be.

You've also observed the top performers in your industry, and you've probably wondered, *Are these people smarter or more talented than me?* The answer is "NO!" In fact, they started out just like you did—one sale at a time. But they have advanced, and faster than you have because they've made key adjustments in their daily schedules and lives.

Every sales-generating business consists of largely the same kind of actions: marketing, time management, money management, networking, business planning, lead generation, and the list goes on. How these same items are both organized and executed determines which of us will excel and which of us won't.

Now I know you may be skeptical, because the difference between top performers and most other sales staff seems so vast. It can't really be that simple can it? I know for a fact that it can.

Think about the difference between their results and yours. Do they close ten, twenty, maybe even fifty times the deals you close in an average month? Yes, they do. Yet we all have exactly the same amount of hours in the day.

Don't fall into the trap of thinking they get so much done because they have help. At one time they didn't have anyone working for them, and yet they still outpaced you. The truth is just as you have suspected all along—the top producers know something you don't. They know it's about attitude and belief. These are the things you can't see on the surface, but they are the difference in their business versus yours.

*The top 2% know who they are and
what they want.*
~ Dean Philpott

Getting to Know You

THE FIRST STEP in elevating your business to a new and more productive level is to question everything— and I mean everything. You have to redefine who you are, what you want, and most importantly what success means to you. Start by asking yourself, *Why am I here?* Be as specific as possible and don't think about money. You can make money in any other field in the world, and it would probably potentially be much easier, but you chose your specific field. *What is your why?* What attracted you to this career? Was it personal interaction, helping people, building a business as an entrepreneur, etc.?

You must have a purpose; otherwise you are just doing time until something better comes along.
~ Dean Philphot

Your original motivation is crucial because it's actually the "Why" that drives our results. Earning money isn't a destination or result. It is a commodity that allows you to live the life you want. Maybe that's the freedom to be your own boss, travel, or provide your family with a better life, but money itself can never be the "Why." Otherwise, you'll never enjoy real happiness.

The second question you must answer is *What do I want?* This goes to the core of what success means to you as an individual. We each have different definitions and figuring out your definition is critical. To me, Earl Nightengale has it right when he said, "Success is the progressive realization of a worthy ideal." Success is something that should excite you, something you dream about and want to work for passionately. When you think of success in this light, you focus on what you consider to be your own worthy ideal. It may be building a company or it may be earning enough each year to spend more time with those you love. Whatever your ideal is, that is your worthy goal. Be as specific as you can, and don't worry about how you're going to get there—we'll tackle that in a future segment. For now, just dream.

In order to succeed, you must be able to answer three questions: 1) Why are you doing what you're doing? 2) Where you are right now? and 3) Where do you want to go? Once you have answers, you can create a clear path from one point to the other.

After determining what you want, you must unleash your imagination. I want you to really think about what your life might look like when you achieve your dream. In fact, this is your first challenge. Sit in a quiet room and just visualize. How would you dress, act, and with whom would you associate? What kind of car would you drive? What would your office look like? How would your home life be? What about vacations? Where would you go, what would you do?

Now I want you to close your eyes and imagine yourself existing in that world. How would it feel? Write it down and reread it often.

You must start accepting the reality that the life you want is yours to design. Much like when I was young child, and I didn't think I could become wealthy, because I imagined those people with money to be very different than me, I didn't take the steps to make it happen. Once you understand that you can absolutely have the life you want, you can take meaningful strides toward that goal.

Some find goal setting to be a tedious process, but that's mainly because they haven't done the hard work of figuring out their motivation or exact goals. However, goal-setting is mandatory because it forces you to make solid decisions. Each path is an active choice, and clear goals make those choices much easier.

Every single platinum level producer takes the time to set goals and considers it an important part of their ongoing success strategy. They take the time to make daily, weekly, monthly, and yearly goals as well as long-term, multi-year goals. If people at the top are doing it, it makes sense that those wanting to bring more opportunity into their lives would do so without question. Yet you'd be surprised how many people actually resist setting clear goals. Goals mean committing and committing means risking failure. When people get sidetracked by this fear, they find every excuse not to set goals.

Goal Achieving

REMEMBER: THERE ARE two things we need to know in order to see success: Where we are and where we are going.

Goals raise our current level of awareness. They direct us and give our lives meaning. A goal should be so BIG that it **excites** and **scares** you in the same breath.

Good Goals Must Be...

Clear and Specifically Defined

Achievable in a Given Time Frame

Commitment to Steady Progress

Short and Long Term Goals Aligned

Flexible.

Your Life Began With Goals

You have been a proud young achiever since the day you were born. It is human nature to set and achieve goals. Think of a child, learning to crawl, then walk, then run—they attract whatever kind of assistance they require to achieve these milestones, and they are relentless in this process. The human being is a goal-seeking organism. When you were an infant, you had goals, and you attracted whatever assistance you required to achieve those goals. Growth and change were the order of the day from the moment you drew your first breath. The same creative state can be entered and enjoyed every day of your life.

Materialistic Goals

Materialistic goals have a negative association, but I actually encourage them. Money and things have the ability to make you comfortable, and often the more comfortable you are, the more creative you will become. Consider Maslow's hierarchy of needs—once your basic needs are met, you can put your magnificent mental and creative capacities to work on achieving many things beyond your basic survival requirements.

See It And Want It...

When you are choosing your goal, the only prerequisite is:

You must be able to see yourself on the screen of your mind, already in possession of the goal, and you must seriously want it.

~ Dean Philpott

At the beginning, you **do not** have to know *how* you are going to get it. You just have to know *what* you are going to get. Remember, the proper goal will give you the motivation you need to grow in awareness.

Awareness Gives Meaning To Life

The awareness you are seeking requires replacing a certain amount of old conditioning, which is genetic and environmental. This is a life-long process for nearly every living person. Conditioning is a multitude of ideas and behaviors which are fixed in your subconscious mind and are commonly expressed as habits. These habits are causing the unwanted results you are presently experiencing.

To successfully replace these limiting ideas and habits, you must have a positive goal. Negative habits, if broken and not consciously replaced with positive habits, will be replaced almost immediately by other negative habits. Nature abhors a vacuum. To be successful in replacing negative habits with positive ones, you must have a good reason. That good reason is a goal.

Whenever you have been successfully improving habits in the past, you have either consciously or unconsciously set a goal. The greater the desire to reach this goal, the easier it is to break free of past conditioning and burst through your old paradigms.

"Do the thing and you will get the energy to do the thing."

~ Ralph Waldo Emerson (1803 – 1883)
American essayist, lecturer, and poet.

Attitude

If you're wondering what goal achievers know that you perhaps do not, it is this: your attitude is the composite of your thoughts, feelings, and actions. Your attitude is everything about you. It is not just your thoughts; it is not just your feelings; it is not just your actions. It is the composite of all three. The way you think and the way you feel affects the way in which you behave—and guess what? This affects your results.

"To believe in the things you can see and touch is no belief at all, but to believe in the unseen is a triumph and a blessing."

~ Abraham Lincoln (1809 – 1865)
the 16th President of the United States

Becoming aware of your attitude and how it affects your behaviors will become a critical element of your success when goal achieving. You can start by reflecting on the power of your feelings and thoughts, and how these influence your behaviors. My message is to encourare you to explore your feelings, and the ways that we numb ourselves against them. My hope is that you will unleash the possibility of your conscious feelings and transform your lives into what really matters to you. Can you see how this aspect of your personality have a direct impact on your results?

Thoughts -> Feelings -> Actions -> Behaviors and Habits = Results

Ask yourself: What **thought** could I change today that might change my behaviors for better results?

Organization

A PERSON OR business will not progress with sustainability until they have mastered the art of being organized, both inside and out.

Advance Decision Making (ADM): The ability to make a decision in advance of the actual decision. Sound confusing? This is just a fancy way of saying you need to decide what you will stick to before any stressful situation arises.

For me it was giving up my most enjoyable meal of the day...breakfast. Bacon and eggs were a lifestyle choice of mine for 25 years until my doctor told me I **must** quit this habit if I were to live a longer life! I had to make the decision in advance to say "No!" before I was faced with the question of, "Good morning Dean, your regular bacon and eggs today?" It's much more difficult to make the right choice when you're staring at the situation in the face and have to decide on the spot.

Your old habit kicks in and you reason with your logic to say to yourself, "Well I suppose just one more won't hurt me since I am here with a good friend etc...." Have you ever experienced this kind of inner dialogue?

You will have to make advanced decisions about what kind of schedule you can commit to, what kind of clients you want to interact with, and what actions you'll prioritize.

Until you can commit to being organized, you will be capped at a certain level and will be like Moses, who wandered in the wilderness for 40 years without a hope of ever getting out.

Let's Imagine For A Minute...

You are an Olympic competitor in the game of sales and you need to improve your schedule if you are to win the gold medal.

Tips

THE FOLLOWING ADJUSTMENTS have worked for me, and while everyone is different, committing to a routine will bring positive changes. I trust you will take time to review and see which apply to you.

On Sunday night, I set my schedule for the week. This helps me focus on my clients and prioritize my days.

I also Time Block, which means I schedule my day quite strictly. For me it's the morning that sets the tone for the rest of my day.

I wake up religiously at 5 AM, then meditate and write about gratitude in my journal. I like to be aware of my victories and the role I played in them as well as see the many wonderful people and clients who brighten my day.

After I journal, I make sure to read something inspiring. For those of you needing a new great read, consider picking up my book, an international bestseller called, *Stop Wishing, Start Winning*!

I take the hour between 6 AM and 7 AM to do my workout routine, 7-8AM is my AM family time and breakfast and 8-9AM.

I study my industry. I want to know what other business coaches are doing on their websites, what seminars colleagues are holding, and what home prices are looking like in different areas. This helps me stay on top of my game.

Remember, routine is critical!

It's Your Office, Your System

You also need to set yourself up for success, and this means taking care of the little things like your office and work area.

Lets Talk About Your Office

Does your office make the right impression? Or does I leave room for others who do not kinow you well to question who you are, how you run your business and how to gauge the productivity possible in response to your commitment of service to them?

Are your business and personal goals visible? Show the world what you want—it becomes contagious and builds repiore.

Let's Talk About Your Organization

Is your office organized enough that a colleague can walk into it and find a file within 30 seconds? This type of organization not only helps you work more efficiently, but it also sends a message to everyone around you that you're committed to excellence.

The "Et al" Tips Of Our Industry

When it comes to communication, it is essential you understand sometimes you are not as heard as you think you are. That's why delivering clear and simple instructions should be one of your strongest qualities along with your ability to listen. You have two ears and one mouth for a reason... you can't listen with your mouth open! This may seem like a quirky, outworn cliche, but it still makes sense.

Client Relationships

HAVE AN INITIAL in-person intake session, and take plenty of notes for future reference. You will gain favor with your clients when you are able to respond with ideas, products and services that are in direct alignment with what they have told you they are really looking for. You will also save vast amounts of time in the event you find them shifting into a panic-buying mode.

You may find yourself feeling at some point in time, *It's just not working!* If you have studied Communication 101, you will know the next best step is to simply ask a question from the relationship test and be authentic...On a scale of 1-10 how would you rate our working relationship?

What will have to happen for us to get to a 10?

Powerful questions, right?

Life And Balance

ONE OF THE hardest things for assertive sales people to understand and implement is life balance. For many of us, and I include myself here, it seems that life is a cycle of working really hard, playing really hard, and having great relationships... but for years, I couldn't figure out how to have them all at once! It seemed if work was going well and sales were off the charts, I didn't have a minute to spare for my family, or myself, and the reward I got was exhaustion! My relationships and personal well-being

125

suffered greatly during those times. However, when I finally got a handle on my relationships and was well-rested, my business seemed to stall a bit. I almost became convinced that it just wasn't possible to have it all.

It took me years to understand that I **could** have it all, and I learned how to blend an equally successful work life and personal life in a way that worked for me. However, the principles I'm sharing aren't new. It just takes balance.

As humans we have many physical, emotional, social, and spiritual needs. While you may think that you are different and can simply skip some of them, I'm here to tell you... you can't. Suppressing or denying your needs leads to a completely imbalanced life, and this will eventually destroy what you are trying to build.

Don't think I had this figured out from the start... I didn't figure out most of it until I was past 40! I think perhaps there is something about age that makes you more reflective, but that doesn't mean someone can't come along and shorten your learning curve.

I was fortunate when Robin Sharma a Canadian writer, motivational speaker, and leadership expert, introduced me to the idea that there are eight forms of wealth—not just one. The new perspective changed me and allowed me to embrace many of the aspects my life was lacking. Since then, I have been a much happier, healthier, and more successful person.

The idea of wealth that was seated deeply in my mind seemed always to have a big price tag attached. I thought someone who was wealthy surely must have had either a hand out or a head start. But I came to realize there is wealth in every aspect of life and money is only one very tiny part of it. Because I had these preconceived notions about wealth, I could never imagine myself as wealthy; it was completely foreign to the way I viewed my life and abilities.

However, I now know wealth is so much more than a bank balance. A wealthy person is at peace with who they are and can see beyond mere monetary gain. A wealthy person always values people above and beyond anything, including money. They can slow down and breathe in life, or speed up, embrace opportunities, and make conscious and active choices. They are reflective and value all opportunities, even small ones, to improve themselves.

Although Robin Sharma notes eight forms of wealth, I want to talk about just three of them here in my conclusion.

Inner Life

Your inner life is what goes on in your mind. You become what you think about, and you reflect how you view yourself. A significant truth is this: your outward life can never be bigger or better than your inner life. I didn't have much money when I was younger, and this was because I didn't view myself as the kind of person who was wealthy. I didn't even consider it a possibility, so I made no attempt to achieve it.

An inner life is being able to step back and view the kind of person you are and what you want to become. It is being able to make conscious choices about how you want to conduct your life each day. This includes choosing to **respond** to daily turmoil rather than just **reacting**. It is a more thoughtful approach to life. My morning meditation allows me to empty my mind and just listen. We each have the solutions to all our problems within us, but if we never take the time to calm our minds and allow that creative energy a space to exist, then we lose it.

Your Challenge: This week spend 20 minutes at the beginning of each day completely alone in a quiet place. Close your eyes, relax and breathe in to release all your pent-up energy. Allow this state of peace to wash over you. After one week, write about the differences you feel in your life.

Your Health

Most of us think health is eating right and exercising, and it is, but it's more than a quick trip to the gym or having a salad instead of a burger. Feeling good impacts every other part of your life and this includes your emotional state, ability to focus, and even how you feel about yourself. It also releases a great deal of creative energy.

In order to maximize the benefits, you must find a form of exercise that suits you. It might be as simple as a walk in the park, or it may be running, swimming, or biking. It really doesn't matter what you do; just do something!

I decided a few years ago to start eating better— nothing major. I just cut out most of the processed and fast foods and started running. I now run three miles, five times a week, and my creativity has exploded. I will say this was the last aspect of the eight forms of wealth that I implemented, simply because I've always dreaded exercise, but now I actually look forward to it. When your body is fully engaged in exercise, your mind is free to take flight!

Your Challenge: This week I challenge you to improve your diet—it doesn't have to be drastic but maybe just skip the fast food lunch or that morning donut that tastes so great with your coffee. Make the decision **right now** that at least three times this week you will exercise.

Your Family

Each of us has a family. We have people whom we love and who love us. While this may or may not look like a traditional family, it is your modern family and that can have any definition you wish. Family provides a core energy and purpose to what you do. My family includes my two children, and they are the definition of unconditional love, but even so, just like any valued relationship, it takes work.

Families are held together by shared traditions and expressions of love. My dad was a big believer in traditions and every Dec. 24th we would all gather to look at Christmas lights, and though it was a very small thing, it brings back some of my fondest memories. We just lost my dad, and in the final moments of his life his entire family surrounded him. I realized what a very wealthy man he was because in the end nothing else matters quite like the love he must have felt.

Your Challenge: Create a healthy family life. This may be creating your own tradition with your modern family or simply picking up the phone and reconnecting with a loved one.

As you incorporate each of these ideas and suggestions, you will experience the beginning of a balanced and fulfilling life.

I want to take this opportunity to thank you all sincerely for being a part of this book, I mean that because you are the reader and it's because of YOU that I do what I do. It is because of the people I serve I have learned to be Abundantly you! on purpose in business.

About The Author

Bringing incredible real estate and sales experience to the table, including many years as Yukon's top producing realtor, Dean Philpott is the author of the international bestselling book, *Stop Wishing, Start Winning.* A proud father and extreme lover of life and adventure, Dean's company operates globablly with offices in Whitehorse, Yukon and Nanaimo, British Columbia.

Dean is currently a highly sought after business and real estate coach as well as writer and public speaker. His program, *20 Minutes to Platinum*, is a breakthrough live training event designed to jumpstart realtors into highly successful habits in as little as 20 minutes per day. When Dean isn't working on his empire, he's playing the guitar or taking private pilot lessons.

Contact:
dean@deanphilpott.com
http://www.philpottseminars.com/20min/
http://www.philpottseminars.com/

Other books by this author:
http://www.amazon.com/Stop-Wishing-Start-Winning-Philpott/dp/1599303965

The Energy Of Success

Bringing Success With You

Valerie Sorrentino

"Often, it's not about becoming a new person, but becoming the person you were always meant to be, already are and are dying to express.

~ Valerie Sorrentino

There is a myth that "business is business," and that somehow corporate executives and entrepreneurs become someone else—sharks or drones—when they step into their offices. In truth, the most successful business owners feel free to express all of who they are, lovingly connected, at home with themselves, empowered and confident from the inside out. It is the journey of becoming abundant, and building a business of purpose, on purpose, that makes it possible.

The Disguised Spiritual Journey

HAVE YOU HEARD of the spiritual journey disguised as a business? I hadn't heard of it. I hadn't even heard of a spiritual journey when I was all wrapped up and involved in our family business. Owning a building and staffing our restaurant felt nothing like a spiritual practice to the naked eye. My husband and I were working hard, our other partners were toiling at full capacity—we were all working and praying a lot, but that's about as spiritual as it got.

I'd put the clairvoyant side of myself away years earlier to be a much more upstanding citizen, parent and business owner, until one day, I had just had it! I spoke my truth. I walked into my husband's office at a very bad time. *No time would have been good for this particular conversation*! I spoke evenly, clearly and with precision in that moment, and spirit started to carry me into a whole new direction of prosperity and wealth!

Ok—so it didn't happen as easy as all that! But the day I actually gave my husband my two-week notice of resignation was the day I began to build an abundant life for myself. It's not that I didn't have a choice. Our partnership had always been a great one. And being partners with other family members had been a way of life for... about a lifetime. Yet the day I finally stepped into the truth of my words, aligned with the truth of my heart— with the courage to stand exposed in truth—is the day I started owning my life.

It was just not a "moment in time;" this day and every single day continues to be better, happier and richer for myself and my family.

The Hard Part – Getting Real

BUT HERE'S THE hard part. It was time for me to start owning other areas of my life and get vividly clear about what was important to me and what was not. Running a thriving, successful business is important, of course. As an entrepreneur, running a business is built into the DNA. But for me, I wasn't truly running my own business in the 80's and 90's. I was working in our business. There's a difference.

From that moment of truth until today—and I suspect each day moving forward—being an Entrepreneur and a successful business owner became absolutely, explicitly a spiritual, abundant and prosperous journey on purpose!

Funny, because I thought I was speaking my whole truth when I gave notice that day. I thought speaking the truth was all it would take. My husband was stunned. He was in shock that I could possibly not want to remain there in our incredible restaurant and serve our incredible friends, family and the hundreds of people who walked through our doors... meal after meal every day and night. It wasn't that.

It wasn't that at all. I just had a part of me that was ready to be expressed; a deep, intimate part I was otherwise afraid to reveal. The part of the truth that I found the hardest was revealing my true identity. I was partly in a state of denial and partly in a state of bliss about being exposed as a healer, an energy worker, and an expert in knowing that our environment has everything to do with our wealth,

135

health and happiness. I was going to have to take a stand the only way I could express the work I was doing, and say, "I help your mind and body with my heart, and it's kind of invisible, but it will help you, because it helped me heal."

Back then, there was only one thing that was absolutely clear to me—deep down inside I had more to give. My heart was calling me to make a difference in the world. I had to take a stand and take a step out on my own. And it might be cold and windy out there on the streets of solo-entrepreneurialism. Sounds dramatic, doesn't it? It was. I did it anyway!

Thankfully it wasn't as scary as all of that and here's why: I felt centered, I felt clear, and I felt supported in the ability to speak words of truth. That began to make more sense than hiding behind words of resentment or confusion or disdain for the hard hours I was working.

When I stepped out in my own direction I was standing tall and I was standing in unwavering faith in my mission. Then there was that moment of trepidation when I thought, *Now, all I have to do is figure out what my mission actually is.*

Today, I coach, mentor and teach transformation to high-achieving success-oriented people who are in the midst of knowing there's something more. The way to inner peace is a proven path. And that path might very well be into the heart of your business. But, more possibly, it starts somewhere else. What if you don't work for yourself, or you are holding a position at a job you know is right for you in many ways, but there is something dragging you down? What then? You know something's got to change, but you are clueless about what. This is for you, too. Happiness and abundance is for everyone; it's here for us all.

As an energy worker since May of 2001, I've learned so many levels of balance it is often dizzying. This is why getting to know your true self is truthfully where it all begins. Creating the space of abundance and living a prosperous life can be so much simpler than you think. It actually happens in everyday life right where you are. Right now!

I suppose the reason business is known as a spiritual journey is because in order to experience true success you must be deeply connected to your inner truths, inner voice and gut instincts in order to glide through the highs and lows.

As high achievers, every day we face fears, demons, and the images of our wildest dreams. We face defeat, triumph, and our worst nightmares. We dig deep, find strengths, act in faith and ask for mercy. We come to conquer giants against all odds. We give in, we give hope, we receive in uncanny ways and we care so deeply inside of us that the ache to succeed and make a difference in the world drives our every waking thought. We are the heart-centered entrepreneurs and change makers.

We must connect compassionately and with purpose with our clients, staff, vendors and purveyors . We make a difference in the world and in the lives around us by tapping into our own personal strengths. When we offer these strengths we reveal business as a new breed; a new classification: the *Heart-centered Entrepreneur*/CEO.

There's an ingredient to success today that plays an essential role in the life and times of the heart-centered entrepreneur. The world now experiences many Empaths, Change Makers and Highly Sensitive People (HSP); each is subject to the demands of the new paradigm, but have certain needs to consider.

In order for Entrepreneurs to achieve, experience and exemplify true success to the world, we each must pay close attention to a place beyond the office, a place beyond the conference room. We must pay tribute to the essential zone it all comes from—where success happens for the modern *heart-centered peace and love generation,* during our waking hours and our restful nights—and that place is the place we call *home.*

Home is the sacred space where true success is cultivated from the inside out. Inside the mind and body. Inside the heart and home. And, yes, inside the office, too. There are spaces that need our undivided attention in all facets of life.

These new spaces, which are rather invisible at first, are really vast, enormous and powerful. The space is intimate, vulnerable and sweet. The space is found between the ears and connects deeply in the heart while it's offered out into the world through the eyes, lips and the hands. This space manifests around us everywhere we go.

Yes, work can be exhausting. Work is work—long hours, with many needs and demands are nothing new to high achievers. We give, we create, we negotiate. We build, we travel and we bring home the bacon.

And Then We Go Home

THERE'S THIS PLACE called home. We find our peace, and the next day we go out and do it all over again.

Some of us hard workers will get into a nicely defined "the same old thing," kind of a grind, and even the lovely sounding "heart-centered" ones can work themselves to the bone if not watched after. It all sounds so nice and loving to come from the heart and connect authentically. It also takes a keen eye and an open ear to stay in tune with the depth of our soul's mission. And that can be exhausting.

Connecting with one's life purpose can be one of the highest fear-rendering missions on the planet. We risk exposure, defeat and humiliation. What if we don't find it? What if we make a mistake? Heaven forbid!

Well, mistakes are welcomed nowadays. In the field of science they're celebrated. A mistake found in the system of a scientific experiment will be one less mistake in the future of said experiment. Hence, problem solved; the mistake becomes the blessing.

Find it now while your business is small and saves a world of trouble later on. And the mistake of excessive work and amplified drive is a blessing in today's world because, you guessed it, it's an alternate route to return home.

The Life Of A Restauranteur

MY BUSINESS HISTORY went something like that as a restaurant owner and operator. We worked in our restaurant night and day. Every day of the week business came first. There were never enough hours in a day or days in a week. Vacation was a pipe-dream. We had a happy life, but something was missing for me and it showed.

Each day, the spiritual journey of connecting with the soul of your business is there waiting for you, whether you recognize it or not. Sometimes, it feels fruitless and at others... rich and satisfying. Each day is unique. Each day is ripe with potential, but the unknown truth emerges no matter what. It's truly beyond your control and to strive for success can rule every waking moment, if you let it.

But one must rest. Is it possible that one can Relax into Success?

~ Valerie Sorrentino

Three Simple Keys

IN THIS CHAPTER, we address three simple keys. I make that promise because the spirit and energy of the heart in a business has millions of veins leading in every different direction imaginable. It can boggle the mind and keep you up at night. It can dampen the spirit and drain the best of intent. To improve the health, vitality and longevity of your business, let's keep it simple.

Always Keep It Simple

IN KEEPING IT simple, I know my intention. I know what I work for and from. I've evaluated my driving forces, boundaries and must-haves. I continue to check in with myself to see if I'm even close to my own truth at a core level. Clearly defined intentions matter. My intention to simplify has saved my life and the life of my heart-centered businesses, my transformational teaching practice, my life/work balance coaching service and being a mom and a wife of over 25 years... and has done so time and time again. Simplifying life and business and keeping things in balance has kept me sane and kept me successful. It can do the same for you.

How do you keep it simple? I will cover a few simplifying standards and write briefly about the energy of simplicity, the energy of abundance and your personal energy itself. Evolving Heart Centered, Empathic, HSP (Highly Sensitive People) make up our environment today as well as each and every other category of person out there, including CEO's, CFO's,

Chief MOMs, Stay-at-home Dads, you name it! We're all in business to achieve success.

It used to be all about the money. There was a time when money was equated with success. Now we know there is even more to the equation. There is one very real component.

The newly reconginzed element of success, which we cannot live without, is *true happiness*. But the question is, where do we find true happiness in business?

True happiness is the gold strike of successful living. Not just money, not just objects and not just fame. There are no guarantees in business, so how do we guarantee happiness?

Is it included in the work you do?

Is there an abundance or a deficit of the happy factor where you work?

How does one person get some while another stretches and strives for this elusive state?

Remember, it's a bit invisible. But we can see it. We can feel it. We can practically taste it. There's proof that other people have found it. I've seen it and I've discovered where it can be found!

In the promise to keep it simple, let's cut to the brash truth. Happiness lives at home with you. It lives within you and you bring it with you to work. It can sometimes be "found" there but it's most likely not something you can rely upon "finding" but rather, something you bring. You project it. You supply it by demand. It's a must-have in the agenda of life. Happiness is a must. Now—how to achieve this said happiness?

Well, what makes **you** happy?

How well do you know your true, true self? The real you? Have you ever spent any time getting in touch with your deepest inner self? Good, now, take care of that interior. Be kind. Be gentle. Be grateful for all that you are. There's so much to you that you likely don't really know about yourself yet... including your full potential. Not on the workhorse level but on the happy, fun-loving level. You know it... the place in you that comes to the surface when you're totally at ease.

> When is the last time you visited the place of inner peace and ease within you?
>
> Do you bring the sense of peace and ease to work with you?
>
> How do people respond?
>
> Who do you attract?

Ahhhhhh, *ease.* The essence of simplicity has finally come to the surface. Staying at ease.

Where, when and how can you cultivate this place of ease we speak of?

The Place Between A Day's Work

FIRST, I ASK you a question. "Is ease something you intend to have?" As noted earlier, your intention matters. It matters so much so that I'll ask you over and over again what it is that you intend. This helps you keep it simple. Know your intentions and stay clear about them.

Is happiness part of your clear intention? Is it in your business plan? Does a life of ease play a role? I ask because it's never, in my opinion, something to be taken for granted. Nothing important is to be taken for granted in this life. Deep breathing, restful moments, gorgeous sunsets, genuine laughter, an authentic smile... all hold immense power. Intentional simplification... intentional ease... intentional happiness—all have one thing in common—they all take clarity to maintain them; clear intent keeps everything simple.

Let's move on. Let's look at your personal energy and the energy in your home, mind, body and office.

For the success of your business, I ask you, "How does your home feel? Is it in order? Not that it has to be neat and clean 100% of time. But... how is it? Out of order, confused, chaotic, restful, easy to maintain, forgotten, empty, overstuffed, efficient, authentic, comfy or inspiring? Just what is the condition of the place you spend your time between every working/waking hour?"

How's your office? What about your car; what is in your trunk, the glove box, or your garage? Are these places that bring you delight? Can you easily and energetically come and go with pride and joy—in your car, office, home... in your head?

The Place You Call Home

THE PLACE YOU call home is literally the place you retreat to in order to restore the psyche and energy field mentally, physically and emotionally. It is also all tied into the sense of connection to your interests and the ones you love. It's where you feed yourself and prepare your best self to step out into the big exciting world of abundance and success.

Besides making your home a show place for all of the wonderful possessions you want to acquire, how about tapping into a deeper portion of your place and space? Scratch beyond the surface and tap into the soul of your home; the place where you can safely connect to your deeper, truer, more happy self, from the soul of your very being. Ensuring you and your family a safe and healthy environment is paramount to true success. It's a highly validated fact that your surroundings will affect you and your outcomes and reflect your decisions, your desires and your subconscious beliefs.

> *What you see is what you get.*
> *Your environment matters to your business*
> *and your abundance.*
> ~ Valerie Sorrentino

Begin where you are and with what you already have. If you love it or need it... keep it. If you don't... then let it go.

In keeping it simple, as I promised I would, it is time to cover the basic phenomenon that we're

145

influenced by what we look at and focus on. In order to change your world, you must change what you see! In order for your thoughts to become more supportive and be supported by others, shift your inner dialog by changing what you see, hear and say. Create a positive environment and be directly and positively affected by it. It's not exactly something you go to and find... it's something you dream of and then create.

Simply put, what you see is found within you.

In a very strong alignment to this idea—what we see that we don't like is also found within.

Before I began what became a 25+ year study of energy, proper placement and how your personal environment affects your health, happiness and your business, I was in a state of hidden chaos. Although I didn't hide it very well. In my garden, there were prosperously growing weeds and overgrown, well-intended but rotting veggies. Behind closed doors, my closets were filled with laundry and good intentions. I had gone on a search to learn more about energy and balance, yet at the same time abandoned my own natural connection to inner guidance and knowing. The only answer was to go inward.

Don't get me wrong, we were living abundantly... but in all the wrong places. And, to be honest, I didn't realize the shame propagated from within me, while unconsciously creating an environment to support

146

that feeling of shame. It's a classic *which came first* scenario.

Once the kids were born and filled up the adjacent upstairs rooms in our newly built home, I had so much more *abundance* to sort, organize and hide. As much as I tried, I didn't have the knack of systems and order to create a sense of peace at home. To make it easier, my husband wrote out lists for me; to give me a hand, my mother-in-law would come by to help me like it was a wave of a wand... magically putting everything into place. I was trying to do something that felt virtually impossible to do. I was trying to do it all! Something far too many entrepreneurs try to do—and fail.

My space felt in bad shape, as did I. Everything looked fine on the outside but was close to collapsing on the inside.

To make a huge shift, clear your space and create order. Simplify at home. Begin to quiet your mind through some type of meditation. Create a positive living environment at home and allow it to flow into your work.

Stagnant energy can drain everything, including the ability to create money from a sense of abundance and ease.

I made a drastic decision to start fresh, make my home a sanctuary and to clear up any stagnant or draining thoughts going on in my head. Wow, what a blessing! A positive environment on the inside resulted in a direct reflection of the positive growth in my life and my success.

What it boils down to is this: becoming more abundant begins by being more authentic inside and out. To create a place of true support and safety at home is ultimately creating prosperity.

How does this apply to being a success in business? What does this have to do with energy? Let's get back to the place in between work... *home.*

I could clearly see my misalignment way back then. I was putting in far too many hours at work, making almost no money in our family business and wishing I could keep my home in better order. My energy was deflated, distracted and drained.

Those Days Are Gone!

IN SEARCH OF the art of better balance, positive energy and proper placement for prosperity, the study of Feng Shui, Meditation, Space Clearing, Energy Balancing and Energy Psychology and Yoga all came in very handy, but you'd be surprised why.

When I began to follow my true passions just by tapping into my own interests, and when I started to pursue the interests I felt I didn't have time for, couldn't afford or were frivolous... magic happened! They brought out happiness from deep within me. Notice my wording, *"bring out happiness from within me."*

Happiness is part of you. It is something to cultivate and grow. But it must be grown from fertile ground... a home built to support your ability to rest, to renew, and to reinvent.

~ Valerie Sorrentino

Let's just cut to the chase! Home is where the heart is. Are you aware whether your heart feels nurtured, comforted, understood and respected in the place that's responsible for refueling your energy? If not at home, then where? Is there a space to put each object away or in a place of honor? Are the many things accumulating in the cabinets, baskets and countertops? Are loved items displayed or stuffed away and forgotten?

Take note because this may be a pattern. The pattern that is also present at work. Remedy it inside—at home—and it will pay off in spades.

Overwhelm is overwhelm and you will recognize it as a reflection of your closets or your work hours. Both are quite the same and could actually be a habitual condition.

Is there an order to your space? Is there spaciousness to your life container? Can you breathe? Grow? Give, dream and receive from your heart in your home? Is it welcoming?

Too much or not enough and a lack of order can all be quite draining to the energy system of any ablebodied person, even those with the best of intentions. When business is going strong, and work is on a roll, home is a nice place to be able to lay your head to rest.

And when work is slow, times are lean and out of nowhere looms yet another challenge... home is a nice place to come and lay your head to rest.

In other words, at the end of the day, there must be a retreat; a balance of energy between work and home.

An energy shutdown at home, such as a deep need to stay in bed, to oversleep, or vacate the premises may not be a symptom of too much work, it may actually be a sign of not enough energy flowing at home and from your heart. A heart-based business and heart-centered businessperson must connect consciously within the heart in order to thrive. Where does it show up? At home! This lack of passion will inadvertently affect your work, business and profitability.

Gosh, is this stressing you out? Well, that's the point. Stress at home is a factor you want to minimize in order to create a welcoming oasis for your dreams. Isn't that what work is all about—your off-time? Living abundantly is by no means a number in the bank account. That's part of the equation, but the other part is a happy home life with friends, family and great healthy fun. Let's talk about gaining energy and feeling fresh.

Cultivating Impeccable Self Care

FEELING FRESH INSIDE and out... In the ideology of simplicity and success, it's imperative to have an overall view of not only your business plan, but of your whole life-picture. What does this crystal clear picture of your happiness and your success include?

There's one skill this fabulous new level of success and happiness depends upon! This skill is the cornerstone that has the power to save your life, your work and your health. It will help in every relationship. Each and every day will be affected by the mastery of this one particular skill. It's an art, really.

Some people make it look easy. Each person climbing the ladder of success might think they will find it at the top. And there may be a little bit of truth to that on some level, But you can have it on every level if you work at it.

It looks like what success would look like. It feels abundant. To master this skill, you must start now. You must practice regularly, and it must be done at home... where your heart is. In your office...   where your heart is. With your loved ones... where your heart is. And each place you find yourself connecting in to your heart. To be a true success and to live abundantly on purpose in business, authentically, it is essential you master the skill of ***relaxation*** throughout your day.

Business can take up your whole mind and body... every second of the day. Each waking thought can be eaten up your whole life long, if you let it. The words for keeping it simple at home and at work are: *relaxation and ease on purpose.*

You must self-impose disciplines in your own thinking and habits just as you would place boundaries on taking calls in the middle of the night or deliveries on weekends. Your boundaries are set up to work *for your life. It's your life and you are the boss.* Thus, the overall view of your successful life plan is a very dynamic piece to the energy of success. *Be very clear about it.*

To keep things simple, let's keep with a short list of things to consider:

Your **business vision** as a part of your life vision.

Your **life** has room for more than just work, work, work.

The **space** in which you're standing, sitting or sleeping plays an important role in supporting you on every level of your true success.

Having a strong sense of your own **energy** increases the energy of those around you.

Taking care of yourself will help others increase their ability to succeed. As a businessowner, self-employed or stay-at-home parent, you can always use strength around you. Remember, it begins from within.

Being positive helps your energy and being negative drains it.

152

Restoring your energy on a regular basis means it's part of your job. Take time every day. Get good at it. Become great! It takes time to do anything that's important. If it's truly important, you'll get it done and you'll find the time to do it. So, for the sake of your own business plan being accomplished and keeping yourself intact for an extended period of time, plan for ease each day. It starts at home. It lives between your ears and it comes through at work.

For a time, self-care was only addressed when there was no other choice. But self-care is paramount in the formula for a successful business model. Self-care includes but is not limited to:

Quiet time

Introspection

Being in nature

Listening within

Skillful and regular relaxation

Laughter

Beauty

Meditation...

The list goes on. There is so much more, like giving yourself permission to do what you want to do.

Try new things; follow your heart.

Move the body and steady the mind.

Speak your truth clearly and kindly.

Sit quietly and enjoy the peace and quiet.

Know who you are.

Find a teacher.

Be held accountable.

Enjoy your process.

To be abundantly you in business—on purpose—is to live your values and share your innermost self, giving others permission to do the same. Love yourself through this transition. Breathe deeply into your heart. Intend and expect ease and flow. Speak truthfully and create a safe space to be heard. This begins at home and shows up in work. In play. In Love. Being abundantly you undeniably helps you and your business thrive. This revolution is a quiet one. But it can change the world.

About The Author

As an transformational teacher prolific author, healer, spiritual entrepreneur, and speaker, our Valerie Sorrentino courageously rebuilt herself from the inside out—emerging as a lover of inner wisdom, gentle kindness, and truth in transformational processes.

This world-class expert stress relief specialist, who resides in San Diego, California, shares an empowering personal philosophy, "Often, it's not about becoming a new person, but becoming the person you were always meant to be, already are, and are dying to express."

She is renowned in her community as a Relaxation and Lifestyle Expert, using a multi-dimensional approach to well being, powerful personal development and true transformation that touches all parts of life: Mind, Body, Spirit, Home, Health and Happiness—each encompassing Holistic coaching and mentoring for a vibrant and healthy life.

As the founder of Virtual Clarity Vision Board mentoring group, Healthy on Purpose: Natural Solutions for Healthy Living, and Relax into Everyday Success, Valerie continues to spread the word of understanding ones inner calling and clearing the confusion found within through simplified living techniques. A master of using quantum energy to teach virtual courses, and provide in person consulting as well as private retreats, Valerie empowers others to learn the Simple Act of Manifesting in digestible, life changing portions for immediate change to make your world a better place to be.

Contact:

wwwLifeEnergyCoach.com

www.foundationsofmanifesting.com

Valerie@LifeEnergyCoach.com

http://www.valsgift.com/

Other books by the author:

Miracles, Momentum, and Manifestation: Positively DIVINE and Beautifully Abundant

http://www.amazon.com/dp/0991330013

{An} Unsinkable Soul: Waking Up After Depression

http://www.amazon.com/dp/0991330005

Designing a Life and Business

Abundantly Achieved
Through Intention

Anna Weber

*I think 'work' is anything I'm doing with intention
and purpose. There is absolutely no negative
connotation to the word 'work' for me - I feel lucky
that I get to wake up every day and spend my days
doing things I believe in.*

~ Jessica Jackley (1977 -   )
American businesswoman and entrepreneur.

Have you ever seriously considered the idea of being an abundantly you! on purpose business owner, or just what it means to create a business model that supports your living an abundant life? This privilege begins with the way you think, believe and intention your personal and professional goals. A number of things predicate your end results... including having a heart-to-mind discovery of where you currently are in life, the gifts and talents you bring to this planet, and how you purposefully choose to serve the world with them.

It is necessary to pay attention to life as it presents itself to you, moment-to-moment, and then to pay equal attention to the thoughts, beliefs and emotions that either hold you back or shift you forward. The quality of the "attention" you give to life helps you create the quality of intentions and expectations that almost magically bring forth an abundantly you!

How Do You Get There?

WHAT DEVELOPS AN abundantly you! business owner? What a great question on which to focus! When you stop and deeply consider this question, you automatically become more intentional in designing a business model established to bring your best, most-purposeful work to the world. Whenever you give the best part of you, it is a natural consequence you will then have the desires of your heart.

I am blessed to be one of those truly fortunate entrepreneurs who experienced multiple careers, and embraced a wide-gamut of opportunities and emotions. I moved from a 17-year stint as a clothing designer to a bar-certified paralegal probating the estates of people who died in the streets; from a Senior VP of a highly-successful eight-branch mortgage company to a Fiscal Coordinator for a non-profit senior program; and from a strategic planner for major corporations to using those same strategic planning skills as a certified life and business coach for sassy, savvy Entrepreneurs.

Each was what I would call a "good run" of living life and honing my skills, and ultimately—finding my life's purpose as a change agent who helped others have an equally "good run!" I now bear the title, Literary Strategist, and help those same Entrepreneurs claim their own expert status and put their voices in print... to share their poignant and sometimes powerful legacy messages, and ultimately to become highly compensated as they forever leave their mark on the world.

Was each position I held considered a piece of cake, or a journey without growing pains? Absolutely not! More importantly, did each career path provide me the opportunity to claim the title, Abundantly You! business owner? Again—absolutely not. Oh, no! It was only when I started to pay attention to life, moment-to-moment, I was able and willing to realize there is a fairly solid system to follow to become an abundantly you! on purpose business owner; a system comprised of a rather undaunting, small number of sound, easy to understand and follow principles:

Establish goals.

Set strong intentions.

Use essential support tools.

Understand, control, and counter distracting negative beliefs.

Find the "why" that stimulates motivation.

Embrace the process of manifesting a life... desired.

The balance of this chapter, then, is a deeper dive into each of these principles. They have allowed me to embrace my career as an abundantly you! business owner who chooses to serve, purposefully, and in that service, experience the rich rewards of creating a business that supports the lifestyle of my dreams... retired from a corporate setting, running a company that allows me freedom to travel with my husband, and connecting with clients the world over.

Where Does the Journey Begin?

THE FIRST STEP is to stop long enough to have a heart-to-head kind of discussion about exactly what abundance means to you. It might be accumulated wealth, a general sense of overflowing fullness of something you hold essential or valuable in your life, or looking at the term from a spiritual perspective.

This, of course translates to a generally abundant life, which includes expectations of prosperity and health, as well as a unique fullness of life, even when faced with adverse circumstances. Until you know and understand what you are seeking, how will you know when you have found it? Subsequent to having that defining moment, the undisclosed journey continues, with each life choice you make.

You might be interested to know I did not intention my career path of publishing! I loved my life and business strategy coaching and was "slamming" it home with the kind of life and business transformation my clients experienced. I

160

was not prepared for my Creator nudging, well, let's be honest about that... pushing at me—to step into something more purposeful: putting these sassy, savvy voices in print. I remember the day I acknowledged my willingness to embrace a different journey.

There I was, down on my knees in front of my couch, admonishing God, "I simply do not have the knowledge, awareness or skills to take on this task!" He touched on my heart the "how" did not matter; He would get me through all "that!" It was just my task to accept this more purposeful life journey; I was His choice and now... I had to make my own—a decision that matched His!

Be ever mindful each day you are given a renewed opportunity to make a conscious choice about where you set your intentions and level your attention. Unfortunately, when you fail to do so, everything you ignore ultimately fades into a dark passageway of insignificance. In the process, you allow that valuable attention to be distracted by trivialities that bring little or nothing to your life.

Remain mindful you have a daily choice; take in in—internalize it—and be empowered by it!
~ Anna Weber

The empowering results will be found in self-control, positive inner-dialogues, and continued, deliberate forward movement to the abundant business that supports the life you desire.

Establish Goals

Before it is possible to set intentions, it is essential to make the decision for exactly what it is you fully desire in life. To set a goal, you must not only understand what it is you desire to achieve in your life, but the underlying why behind that desire.

There is quite a large difference between the wishes you have in life and those intense, deeply felt desires that are driven by a passion, a why that is bigger than all the obstacles you may subsequently encounter. The mere wishing for an outcome will never be enough to provide the results you desire; it is the commitment backed by intention and attention that supports the manifestation of the desired result.

There is a thread that is interwoven between intention and attention that builds a web of expectation. At the moment you **expect** something to transpire, you are, in essence, underwriting the positive future that is then backed by confidence in, and hope for, the kind of change and success that transmute to an abundantly you! business owner.

Because I initially followed God's design for my life, I did not have the empowerment of a **why** that was filled with excitement and passion. I was however, able to benefit from the three-ply thread of intention, attention and expectation—each undergirded by a strong spiritual commitment that drove me forward, kept me focused, and ultimately... to find the confidence in my purpose and hope for the future it would bring. Today, I stand strong and proud of the voices I have brought to print and filled

162

with a sense of purpose that extends far beyond any **why** I could have created.

Set Strong Intentions

Let me be very clear... to set goals is not sufficient to achieve them! Think about it: each year people make New Year's resolutions on the first day of January and by the end of that month—or at the very latest— the end of February, all thoughts of them have dissipated. If intention and its partners, attention and expectation, have not been engaged, there will not be sufficient strength to achieve any goal. Setting goals is a continuous journey... life is about change, where change is a process of focus and continuous action. Moment-by-moment, as you affirm your intention, you also heighten your expectation and serve to overcome any hesitation or doubt.

Life, as you know it today may not even reflect the results you anticipate when you dream and plan; however, when you add the empowering combination of intention, attention and expectation, you pave the path to successful results. It is a natural... a given— the more you exercise this powerful trio—the more you come to believe in yourself and your desires; a belief that is reflected in positive results.

The intentions I set today are from a place of personal, professional and spiritual commitment. This combination makes it possible for me to remain mindful and purposeful, and extend far beyond ordinary annual business goals. Being a left-brain strategist, this is not to say I don't create my plans and block out time and use all the tools possible from the perspective of strategic planning. They simply do not start at that "level" to expand my life as an abundantly you! (on purpose) business owner.

By going deeper in setting intentions based on my life purpose, every experience is richer and fuller, and because it is more intentional, gives rise to the feeling, on occasion, that I am experiencing that almost magical... abundantly you!

Use Essential Support Tools

There are myriad tools at our disposal in claiming the abundant life to which we are entitled, and interestingly enough, many are found within us! You will find abundance that comes from within, and without limits. Don't confuse this with the financial resources that can, realistically, come with limitations. It is the intention from our soul space, such as giving our time to others—in abundance—that provides pleasure unknown in common hours. Perhaps you have also felt abundant when you offer your compassion to a troubled soul, or let go of judging others. Material abundance—in terms of money and success—also begins within and is stimulated by abundant thoughts, feelings, and creativity as we connect with the inner source of each and the divinity of the consequent expanding abundance.

There are times in my career supporting Debut Authors I have been frightened about financial responsibilities, allowing the "material" elements of money and success to override my thoughts and emotions. These fears did little more than erode my confidence and focus—often causing me to have this erratic pop-corn effect of creating and delivering products and services. It was not a pretty thing!

The more I focused on living my purpose, spiritually, the easier it was to extend my skills and talents, in abundance to those whom I served, and the easier my system supported my process. Overall, opportunities increased, my confidence expanded, and my ultimate hope for an abundant business that supports my desired lifestyle became my reality.

Can You Understand, Control, and Counter Negative Beliefs?

THERE IS LITTLE doubt your beliefs serve to move you forward, or hold you back. Your primary task is to discover them... uncover them! With that awareness, you are empowered to change the beliefs and their impact on your success—in life and business. Sometimes it takes another person to point out your limiting beliefs; you have lived with them so long they do not seem out of place in your life. However, if you are willing to understand just why you react to certain situations, or perhaps how you confront your fears, it is possible to change yourself from the inside out, allowing you to make small, comfortable shifts that align you with more positive intention, attention and expectations. As you shift beyond negative beliefs, you connect deeper and more frequently with your inner power, and over the years... step into it—mindfully and consciously.

Stop and think about the reality: to a certain degree, your beliefs form your attitudes, but... you can choose, in any situation, at any moment, to change your attitude. In the process, you ultimately change your life—most frequently in a positive manner. Discovering and uncovering limiting beliefs can be a difficult task! First, you may not be aware they are limiting, or that they impact your attitude, and in that influence, minimize the conscious choices of intention, attention, and expectation. For example: I was always taught I could push my way through to anything I wanted or needed in life. "Will power—that is the key!" Or was it really the philosophy that "Those who want more, do more?" Perhaps, the daily mantra, "There is no scarcity of opportunity to make a living at what you love; there's only scarcity of resolve to make it happen."

Whichever of these beliefs was imprinted on my brain is not really as important as the fact that it was rarely actually about how hard I "pushed" for something I desired.

Until I was open to discovering the existence of these beliefs, and how they did not best serve me in pursuit of being an abundantly you! (on purpose) business owner—I would never experience the richness life was willing to lay right in my lap... if I would just pay attention to it! Remember when I note life is part of a co-creative process? I do hope I made it clear that co-creation includes you, your Creator and the life God bestowed upon you. Once I was open to letting go of limiting beliefs, what once seemed a never-ending burdensome struggle suddenly became filled with myriad possibilities that miraculously became realities.

Does Your Why Stimulate Motivation?

THE POWER OF knowing your why is always triggered in my mind by the memory of a story one of my clients shared with me. He had a health issue he "could" have managed throughout his life, but for whatever reason, never found anything that mattered enough to help him move through all the challenges it would require... until the day his daughter was diagnosed with an illness in which he could participate as a transplant choice for her, with the exception that his own un-tended issue prevented his doing so.

In one moment, his **why** became so significant... within a matter of weeks he changed what he could never previously find important enough to manage. Only in that moment, when faced with the significant possibility of losing his only daughter did he experience the power of purpose strong enough to tap into every energy he could muster to find the determination and courage he felt he would never find. In that one moment, his mission became clear; his goal was compelling enough to tap into his every potential.

I've found an interesting phenomenon about humans: we need more from life than survival, and without a deep connection to something beyond mere survival, we easily experience disillusionment and a sense of despair. Couple this with the philosophy of Frederick Nietzsche, "He who has a **why** can endure any **how**," and you have the importance of discovering your own **why**.

It is the first step in achieving the kind of goals that are supported by the triad: intention, attention and expectation. I clearly recall the moment I fully understood the financial, educational, emotional and spiritual support of my children was my **why**. As a single mother, it was difficult to work, tend to their needs and attend school, but I was never without the courage to take whatever risks necessary to get ahead.

Today, although they are grown and successful in their lives, they remain my most passionate **why**; just from a little different perspective: I want to ensure the legacy I leave imprints upon their hearts my reality... to stay motivated when challenges arise, continue to pay close attention to life, stay the course when life becomes difficult, and to embrace its challenges in exchange for the potential reward.

While there is no one pathway for discovering your why or your life purpose, there are myriad ways to gain deeper personal insight and a much larger perspective on how your talents can positively change the world, if you will but use intention and attention, and find expectations along the way.

Do You Embrace Life's Manifestations?

IT IS QUITE possible you unknowlingly put up a shield of doubt or discomfort when faced with the topic of manifesting life. What if I told you I once felt the same way? My left-brain just didn't want to budge—not one inch—in the direction of believing it possible to actually "manifest" something I desired in life! It took a lot of reading, studying and observing the actions and results of others around me before I was willing to "shift" just a little bit in my thinking, and, well... limiting beliefs. What did I find? We do unconsciously allow our negative, and sometimes hidden, internal beliefs, dialogs and attitudes to do our "manifesting" for us! And that, my dear reader, can be a travesty!

I learned manifesting is not about attaining material abundance, but is the process of connecting with your thoughts and emotions sufficiently to see moments of being in co-creation with life. In taking advantage of positive opportunities and circumstances in life, working hard at the process of intention, attention and expectation, and in making mindful, conscious choices, we have more of the life we desire. Many people toss around the philosophies behind the Law of Attraction; you may embrace them—you may reject them. I have to interject there is no absolute truth dealth with here; it becomes your truth... the one you must come to from within—as you seek your bigger picture. That expanded picture then becomes your reality... until your thinking magnifies and your picture enlarges again.

Does it all rest in a principle whereby you use your thoughts, intention, attention, and expectation to bring about change, success, and a level of professional and personal abundance that supports your desires?

Do you look beyond Newton's declaration that everything in our lives—in our world—operates as a mechanical universe, and in that observation, consider our thoughts have little to no impact on what we can achieve in life; whatever happens in our lives... we have no influence on it?

I personally prefer the possibility we live in a subjective world of reality, wherein we can and do influence our outcome.

I prefer to perceive the world as one where the external world does look real to me, and although five other people may perceive it differently because they internalized it otherwise, we each create a very personal image of the world from our own minds and hearts. I also believe we experience events as having a beginning and an end, and ultimately, are governed by cause and effect... that cause and effect being stimulated by our intention, attention and expectations.

Life, being a co-creative process, is manifested through your thoughts, beliefs, intention, attention, and expectations. It responds to your inner workings by opening you to situations, events and opportunities in your life—each of which is a direct response to your initial receptiveness to life's possibilities. The events may not present themselves to you in exactly the way you envisioned—that would be naïve thinking—but in your openness to the potential, you will discover how it matches your intention.

What is the Hope?

I TRULY HOPE this chapter inspires you to stop a moment and have a heart-to-head discussion of exactly what abundance means to you. Regardless how you define it, my passion extends to a desire you question enouth to ultimately experience an abundant life, and satisfy your expectations of prosperity and health, as well as a unique fullness of life.

I want to end this Chapter by asking you to consider how you will measure your life. Your response should be a good indicator you will subsequently become passionately and purposefully attached to life; you will pay attention to it, live with purpose and focus your every energy on a why that matters.

Following financial security while following your heart does not have to be problematic; it may simply require a shift in your experience of intention, attention and expectation; it may provide you the experiences to draw more meaning and greater purpose in all you do, think, and feel; and it may compel you to embrace challenges which both stretch and inspire.

"The outer conditions of a person's life will always be found to reflect their inner beliefs."

~ James Allen (1862 - 1912)
A pioneer of the self-help movement.

Do Beliefs Impact Expectations?

YOU BEGIN PROCESSING basic thoughts of building an abundant business—on purpose—with the creation of intentions; you follow that up with the attention paid to what and how you then take action on those goals. Your end results, then will be perceived based on the expectations you hold. Which brings me to the fact that you may have certain underlying beliefs held that may be proven not to be true... now or in the future. It is the continued exploration of your limiting beliefs that can impact your expectations, and ultimately, your end results.

I was shocked as I processed this part of embracing abundance! I came face to face with one limiting belief after another. My stepfather had me quite convinced that no matter how perfectly I completed any task, I should have accomplished it faster, smoother, better... in some manner. My siblings had me equally convinced I was insignificant in our household; small statured, quiet and shy... how could I achieve anything in life? Self-limiting beliefs are like a virus; they expand and are compounded without your awareness. By the time I was married, my relationships were not what they could have, or should have been—the limiting beliefs had grown to a belief I was "unlovable."

172

Work was the only area of my life where I felt there were no limits. What I didn't realize until much later in my journey to an abundant life was that subconsciously, I questioned my right or privilege to abundance and success. I think back on the many opportunities that came my way, but I walked the path... only partway! I seemed always to put a brick wall, just as I was about to bridge the gap between what I desired, and the more deeply embedded lock on my "real" expectations. They were coated in limiting beliefs of which I was not fully aware.

Somewhere along my journey, I realized the path I was really walking; I was tired of feeling broken and unfulfilled. The heaviness in my heart and on my shoulders were no longer acceptable; I set about seeking answers to my questions... directions for my quest.

When you get to this point in your life, you start perceiving things differently; you begin asking different questions, and finally, personal transformation begins and rewards materialize. The problems were not in life around me, but in the life I lived and the limiting beliefs I had dragged along behind me, like a heavy anchor, from one period of my life to another. I have allowed myself the privilege of re-framing the stinging words that broke the spirit of the child in me... perhaps those words were well-meaning at the time, in an attempt to foster the best me I could possibly be. The expectations of others around me inadvertently become my painful truth; at some level, they became self-fulling prophecies.

I believe myself fortunate to have recognized there was something better in life, and that my passion to experience something different was quite high. I courageously sought a different path, and changed my expectations. It was not an easy thing... to break deeply ingrained limiting beliefs. I had to deal with a significant amount of pain. I had to face each and every one, with a fresh new perspective and expectation that beliefs are just thoughts that you keep thinking, which ultimately keeps them active in your mind. The trick was to address them, face them, and remain committed to shift from an old one to something new, something better, and reinforce my thinking with a positive replacement.

Trust me... once you face your limiting beliefs, and begin to see just how disempowereing they are, and separate you from the live you desire... it gets easier and easier to let them go, and shift your future expecations with newer, more empowering beliefs.

I encourage you to embrace this reality: You absolutely have the power to set intentions, engage in the quality of attention to your pursuit of an abundant life, and change what you choose to belive... and what you expect for yourself. I challenge you to accept the responsibility for making your life abundant, and creating a business based on purpose.

About The Author

Anna Weber has long been the "go to" person for debut authors who have a burning desire to be successfully published, but get stalled in the overwhelm and confusion that is the "maze" of the industry. Her authors gain the benefit of her highly expanded understanding of an ever-evolving and complex industry. Many experience her dedication, commitment and tenacity on projects that have unique issues that extend beyond what might require more time and attention.

Contact:

www.SuccessfullyPublished.com
www.VoicesInPrintPublishing.com
aweber@voicesinprint.com

amazon.com/author/annaweber

Other Books By The Author

Miracles Momentum & Manifestation: Unleash the Secret Powers to Having the Life You Desire: Momentum Through Manifesting and Miracles

{An} Unsinkable Soul: Life as I Know It...

BREAKTHROUGH Writing Strategies: Demystifying the Challenges Faced by Debut Authors

Winning the Author's Inner Game (Promoting Your Book On a Shoestring

Discover Your Inner Strength: Cutting Edge Growth Strategies From The Industrys Leading Experts

Dear Reader,

Thank you for reading *Abundantly You! On Purpose in Business!* You were "promised" wisdom and guidelines to initiate change in your life and we believe that promise has been kept. Abundance is a natural birthright, one that incorporates material abundance and a mindfulness of the consciousness of our Creator. Unlike other abundance materials that offer certain "laws" to be followed, Abundantly You! integrated heart-felt stories to which you could relate, and life-changing activities in which you can easily and quickly engage. The steps are clear; the writers' tone pragmatic, yet endlessly enthusiastic. Each story is most decidedly a poignant celebration of entrepreneurship, spirituality, wealth, riches and abundance in all areas, which is what happens when you decide to create financial freedom in life.

Notes: